Pulling Down the Barn

Great Lakes Books

*A complete listing of the books in this series
can be found online at http://wsupress.wayne.edu*

Pulling Down the Barn

Memories of a Rural Childhood

ANNE-MARIE OOMEN

Interlochen Retreat, June 09

Dear Bill —
For your thoughtful perception,
clear insight, honest questions,
tender heart — my sincerest
Thanks + respect.

WAYNE STATE UNIVERSITY PRESS
DETROIT

Anne-Marie

Library of Congress Cataloging-in-Publication Data

Oomen, Anne-Marie.
Pulling down the barn : memories of a rural childhood / Anne-Marie Oomen.
p. cm. — (Great Lakes books)
ISBN 0-8143-3233-1 (pbk. : alk. paper)
1. Oomen, Anne-Marie—Childhood and youth. 2. Country life—Michigan—Oceana County.
3. Farm life—Michigan—Oceana County. 4. Oceana County (Mich.)—Social life and cus-
toms—20th century. 5. Oceana County (Mich.)—Biography. 6. Farmers—Michigan—Oceana
County—Biography. 7. Girls—Michigan—Oceana County—Biography. I. Title. II. Series.
F572.O3O58 2004
977.4'5943'092—dc22   2004006440

ISBN-13: 978-0-8143-3233-7
ISBN-10: 0-8143-3233-1

∞The paper used in this publication meets the minimum requirements of the American
National Standard for Information Sciences—Permanence of Paper for Printed Library
Materials, ANSI Z39.48-1984.

Grateful acknowledgment is made to the Beach Bards of Glen Arbor for the support of the
publication of this volume.

Some of this work was previously published in
Under the Sun
Kinesis
Quarter after Eight
Array
Traverse: Northern Michigan's Magazine
Moon Journal
Green Hills Literary Lantern
Peninsula: Essays and Memoirs from Michigan
and by WIAA, public radio station in Interlochen, Michigan

A portion of the author's proceeds from the sale of this book will go to Fresh Food
Partnership, providing fresh food to people in need.

To my father for telling me stories; to my mother for, as best she could, keeping them (and us) straight; to my brothers and sisters for tolerating my vision of our shared past; and to David, for making it all possible.

Contents

Acknowledgments   ix

First Sound   1

Hay   5

The Hand   8

Apple Gifts   12

First Gods   14

The Barn   17

The Second Fall   22

Killdeer   29

Violence   32

Winter Fields   40

Weather Changes   50

Metaphor   56

Cleaning Kill   64

Interruptions   70

Liturgy   80

Water Jugs   87

Bees   91

The Return   100

Tractor   104

The Witness   115

The Host   118

Pulling Down the Barn   134

About the Author   137

ACKNOWLEDGMENTS

It's not often I have the chance to thank the people who have supported my writing generally and this project specifically. I intend to take full advantage of the opportunity.

My deepest gratitude to everyone at Wayne State University Press, but particularly Annie Martin, the acquisitions editor who first adopted this manuscript. My hero. Heartfelt thanks to my Interlochen colleagues Jack Driscoll, Melanie Drane, Terry Caszatt, Lesley Tye, and Nick Bozanic for their encouragement—and especially Mike Delp—for continuing to push me to submit when I had given up. I'm forever grateful to Interlochen Arts Academy for supporting early drafts of this manuscript through the Writer-in-Residence program and for professional development funds to attend the Bear River Writers' Conference, which got me started again after a long hiatus. My sincere thanks to Deborah Wyatt Fellows, Ellen Terrant, and Jeff Smith of *Traverse: Northern Michigan's Magazine*, and to Norm and Jacob Wheeler at Glen Arbor Sun for publishing early versions of many of these chapters. Thanks also to the Sunday Writing Group—Bronwyn Jones, Gilda Povolo, Stephanie Mills, Dottie West, and Lorraine Anderson—for making me pay attention; to Kimiko Hahn and Patricia Foster, my MFA advisors at Goddard College, who nursed a fragmented collection toward narrative; to the first readers of this leaner version of the manuscript: Kathleen Stocking, Annie Stupka, Jim Schwantes, Geoff Peregrine, and especially Mike Steinberg; to the Stone Coast Writers Conference family, especially B. Lee Hope, Steven Dunn, Laure-Anne Bosselaar, Patti McNair, and Eric May; and to the following organizations for supporting the development of my writing: Glen Arbor Art Association, Land Information Access Agency,

Michigan Writers, Inc., Michigan Land Use Institute, Old Town Playhouse, and Northwestern Michigan College's Extended Education Lifestory Writing Program. Finally, thanks always to the Beach Bards and the Sauna family for listening to stories of my childhood; and to Jeanette Mason, Pauline Tyer, Ruth Nathan, Betsy Eaton, Jackie McClure, Steve Morse, Walter Elder, Dana McConnell, and Sharon Randolph for, in one critical way or another, being transformative in my development as a writer. Thanks most of all to the Oomen family.

First Sound

She is an old hill of a woman, leaning against the sewing machine, singing softly in a language I cannot understand. Her once ample body slopes from the shoulders down, inclining into drooping breasts and folds of stomach. Her hands are as faded as late fall, her skin loose and fissured as a poor field. Though I cannot understand it yet, her face is riddled with pain. She is not sewing, nor is she looking at me. She is singing. I am sitting on the floor near her. From the front porch windows, shadow and light fall through thick leaves and shift over us. She looks out at the north fields, toward the barns, toward the crops. She looks at the fields as though they are something she has never seen before, like a wonder of this world. She looks at them as though she is listening or singing along. This is my earliest and only memory of Grandma Josephine Oomen, my father's mother.

I do not know it, but she is dying.

She has come here to our farm in 1955 because her cancer has progressed to the point where my grandfather cannot care for her any longer. On rare days like today, she can lift herself out into this room, the parlor. In the evening, Grandpa Henry Oomen, an old Dutch man with a mustache, will come from his farm, the one he purchased in the first decade of the twentieth century, to this farm, now owned by his oldest son, John. He will eat with us and sit next to her in the bedroom. This farm where we live, where she is dying, is the second that Henry

Oomen purchased in Oceana County, ten miles inland from the coast of Lake Michigan in the state of Michigan. Though the two farms are not quite contiguous, they are set in the same rolling hills south of the tiny village of Crystal Valley and east of the town of Hart. They are the beginning of a legacy that still exists, passed now to the fourth generation.

An earliest memory is something like a flag tying you to a country. For the rest of your life, it waves in your past, emblematic and formative. Because this one memory has to do with sound, it is anthem-like. In that moment in which Grandma Jo is singing in Dutch, French, or perhaps Flemish—another language she may have known—her voice is low and thick. She stops sometimes, breathes against the old machine, murmurs to herself. There is a lot of coming and going in her voice. The light plays over us, sometimes golden, sometimes dark, but it is the sound—hers and the others—to which I am listening.

In that time when I am a girl, sound becomes a looping thread associated first with weather—that ever present creature that could swoop over us, cawing its fierce or lazy language—but also with machinery—tractors and combines and the smaller tools, the drills and welding machines, the whir of the sewing machine, the whine and whoop of work. I learn the sounds of animals: pigs gurgling, cattle lowing; the different notes of the pigeons cooing, hens laying; and the sounds of the house: dull clank of Melmac against a sink's enamel, the regular thud of the washer sloshing its load, the brush of a broom over chipped linoleum, the snap of sheets before folding. Listening through the years, I become discriminating—I know what field is being cultivated, hoed, picked; what machine is being repaired; what room of the house I should avoid; which little sister has scraped her elbow; which dog has been hunting; which hog is feeding in its mud-caked pen. But in my grandmother's voice, this one and earliest voice, singing weakly, I learn for the first time the farm's coupling of love and death.

I keep trying to find more of her. In my mind I go back to that single moment, thinking that if I can place myself into it firmly enough, it will be the center of everything and the just-before and just-after moments will spread out, like cloth soaking up a spill. As each strand is wetted I will have another moment, and I will be able to know myself, the meaning of all the songs of that time.

It never works.

So I try to build something from memory and imagination. I tell myself she has shuffled into this room to ask for a drink of water, that she has lost her way, sat down, knowing somehow that this room leads to the back kitchen where we still have green-and-white checkerboard linoleum. Where there is water. Sometimes I believe I am there because I have been scolded for running too fast. Perhaps she is singing, despite her weakness, because this is the closest thing to comfort she can offer. She can no longer hold me on her lap. I make it up because it seems right, so close I can breathe it.

Grandma Jo comes to the farmhouse in autumn; she dies in March. She dies in the bedroom where my parents sleep both before and again after her illness.

I keep trying to get her back. No, that's not quite right.

I keep trying to get back the moment when I am looking at her and I can feel myself about to understand. Who she is has ceased to matter; it is her attempt to tell me something that matters. I feel again and again that something nearly articulated, a clearing in that weather, meaning— almost. Then it closes over and I can only imagine.

As I grow up and learn the work of the fields, the sounds take on light, weight, intent—like the antiphonal responses I hear in church and to which I will finally be lured. And I learn not just the way we sound or sing when we are close or dying, but how voices and sounds distort. In the distances of fields, sound shears off the body like chaff. It is carried over air in fragments. Truck to field, field to barn, barn to house, coop to well, room to room, body to body. Our voices are thin threads pulled taut and faint over all the other senses. Our sounds are strands woven together. We strain to hear. If we are lucky, we find meaning.

Once, in a field, I look up from picking asparagus to see the light in a hired man's hands cupped around his mouth. He calls clear to the house in elongated vowels: *Waaaaaattttaaaaaaa*. My sister, Marijo, brings the jug right away. I see my mother step beyond the screen door, open her whole body, call *Supper*. We lift our heads from picking, cutting, hoeing, and we go. I hear my father's long calls to the men—*How far? How long?* I hear as I hear storm, or loss, or amazement, and the distant answer back, *'Til dark*. That completeness.

I was so little, sitting there on the floor in front of her, but I believe in my longing to understand. This is what I have of those earliest times on that farm in Michigan. Her voice and face are only the first, and not the most important, of the many images I carry, but the longing to understand is what this is really about. I am trying to hear hers and all the voices of that childhood: the words, the unwords, the other languages, the machines, the fields, the barns and their animals. I am trying to connect again through the inconsistency of memory—a spill of girl, liquid and wet, soaking into the fabric of that time—longing to know what was being said in that childhood on the farm.

Hay

Hot. So hot we wake dreaming of water. Today, we'll haul hay. Because the air is humid, thick with damp, we won't begin at dawn in post-night coolness. We'll begin at ten, when the heat thickens and turns itself inside out with dryness. By that time the sun will have burned the dew off the hay, and in the heat of the day we'll haul the hay. If we don't wait until it's dry, it will mold.

We ride the tractor out, drinking dust with our coffee. Today two tractors, with two wagons behind each one, crawl onto the sixty-acre field. These tractors are like a string of work days in a line—tractor, wagon, wagon; tractor, wagon, wagon. We move like slow worms across the stubble. Rain threatens. We could lose it all. The sky and the field are hot and heavy.

I bend to it, heave the bale to my knee. The strain ripples from my lower back to my neck. I shift the bale to my thigh, swinging the weight against my hip. I carry it, lumbering like an old animal, and heave it up to the wagon, bracing it with my shoulders. Someone on the wagon leans down, catching the twine in worn leather gloves. As they lift from above, I shove the weight off my shoulders. Bales are stacked as neatly as cement blocks. The wagon never stops moving. We don't talk. We never talk during this work. We become reverent without knowing. We know only that it is slow and hot. If asked, we would say only, "Storm's coming."

The sky darkens in the west. It's still hot, but the wind shifts like an old brood mare, her time coming on. Dust sinks into the wet space between my shirt and my skin, and turns pasty. If I scratch, it itches, burns, and rashes up like the edge of a rusty blade. We walk miles, up and down, until we've learned the field like a hard spelling lesson.

The fields of my childhood carry names with the consonants of hard gods: cucumber, zucchini, rutabaga, turnip, potato, carrot, corn, squash. The grains, though their names are somewhat softer, are no less demanding: wheat, rye, alfalfa, soy. Our fields speak a liturgy repeated through seasons, each crop shaping a gospel that recedes in harvest as the next crop rises in planting.

But the most fiery and demanding of the field gods is hay.

The wind gusts, pretending it doesn't believe in itself, moving unpredictably as a bird. The wagon, dangerously full, bulges and sways like a pregnant animal. I ride on top back to the barn, which is nearly as hot as the field—and dustier. The dust rises like fog when the wagon pulls into the bay, enclosed and incestuous, carrying the smell of manure from cattle in the lower barn. My father looks anxiously out the door as the western sky tinges with dark.

I climb off the wagon, stagger to the door, and slide down to the floor of the barn, my back against the barn door, my head resting on my knees. I overhear them talking about me. "Dryhated" is the way one hand says it. He means "dehydrated," but the way he says it is what I really feel. Dryhated. I overhear my brothers inside, talking softly, tiredly, telling my dad I haven't the stuff.

We are in the field again. When the threat of rain is very close, my mother comes out, puts a baby in a crate, and drives the tractor with another child clinging to her from the front running boards. Children are sometimes invisible on farms or, just as often, their individual needs and talents are molded to the needs of the farm. Most of farm life is given over to the animals and fields, but without consciousness. There is no way of life on earth as demanding as the farmer's. It is an unspoken religion; its fields are our gods. If you are born into it you may come to love it, but you will rarely be able to speak the life because it is stronger than you. We give ourselves up to it and never know it.

The hired man who has been driving leaps down into the field, begins hauling bales. We move faster, racing the rain. When the sky takes on a greenish haze, my mother ties the steering wheel in place and lets the tractor roll forward, driverless. When the tractor needs straightening, she jumps from field to wagon tongue to tractor seat. She adjusts the wheel, lines it up with the lone tree at the end of the field, and then leaps back down to the field without stopping the machine. In my dreams it is not these physical feats that haunt me, but the calling that sears my being with cellular knowledge: babies crying, men shouting, old engines growling against a rising wind. And always there is the old hymn of storm.

The Hand

I am so young that the birth of Patti, the youngest of the five of us, is still months away. It is a hot summer night, just before dawn. My upper bedroom, with its loose window panes and faded wallpaper, has flickered with heat lightning since midnight. Marijo, the baby for a few more months, sleeps in a crib in my room, but I, the oldest, am privileged to sleep alone in the big double bed with its curved wooden headboard wobbling a little forward, like dark protective wings. I am not afraid of storms.

This night, wide awake, I imagine I am a warrior queen, commanding that the lightning gather in my sword so I can slay the monster hiding in the big silver maple outside my window. I climb to the foot of my bed, grab the edge of the sheer curtain, and pull it over my face, waiting for the moment when a wizard will return my stolen life.

I am young enough to believe in fairy tales, but at the first serious slam of thunder, I shriek. The silver maple arches in the wind like a wild, many-fingered hand. Sterling streaks tear the night air again and again. The lightning shrills metallic light into the room. Marijo rolls over, opens her eyes, sees my veiled face at the foot of the bed, and screams. Another crack resounds through the air.

My mother thuds up the stairs, at our door almost immediately. The boys run down the hall and burst into the room behind her. She picks up and cuddles Marijo, slips onto the old bed, and begins the soft murmur that has calmed us all through our babyhoods. The boys curl onto the pillows around her. She leans against the dark headboard, and as the storm rises we watch it, for a moment together. She looks at me, the curtain wrapped around my neck, and sighs.

Lightning explodes the yard light, but there is so much flashing that we can see the rain in stop-action, throwing itself down like a giant gray hand pressing on the fields. The barnyard turns into a shallow lake. In the west cornfield we can see the rows of fingerlings fall as the soil around the roots washes away in the flooding. Tom, who is seven, says, "We're gonna lose it." My mother nods. Thunder rolls, thick as a wall.

I have found a small hole in the curtain, and I am sticking my finger through it, making a dancer with a long skirt.

"Washouts!" Rick says, pointing through ashen light. We can see ridges a foot high sheering the clay slope of the low yard near the road. The boys crawl close to the windows, staring, eager, tied to the storm, to the land. The light reaches up like a slow hand, spreading slowly over acres and acres.

My brothers, *these boys*, will inherit the farm. On some level they know this already. Through tradition and expectation, this vista belongs to them now, before they can even read. It belonged to them before they were born. As dawn slides toward us, the lightning moves into the county east of us, but the rain does not stop. The boys watch it as though it is a suspenseful story.

My mother picks up a book from the bed and hands it to me to distract me from tearing the curtain. She has begun to give me books, but, preoccupied with the baby, she reads to me less often now. I open it and play with the words. "One, two . . . bu . . . bu. . . ." I stumble on the "ck" in buckle, and my mother supplies the word, "Buckle, like a belt buckle."

"Oh, a buckle, a buck, buck, buck—like a deer?" I ask, prepared to be silly. I am learning to read. I have begun to make up my own words. I also have so many imaginary friends that my mother worries. I randomly open the book to another page, without words, and begin inventing.

"Once upon a time there was a tree who could talk, and it asked what was in the oven, and the oven said berry berry was in the oven."

Rick stares. Tom snorts.

"Berry, berry, quite contrary, how does your garden grow?" I chant off into my own world until Tom complains, "I can't hear where the thunder is."

They will always want to know where the thunder is. They are stronger, more aware of present dangers than I am. Tom turns back to the window, and the twin towheads press against the window, watching for the next flash of lightning, knowing already the language of weather. While I struggle to read words, my brothers learn to read rainfall and soil and sky. I close the book and watch my brothers as they watch, breathless, the rising of thin dawn light as though it is an answer to a hard question.

My mother, her fine Belgian features perplexed, carefully shifts a dozing Marijo, but she watches me anxiously as I meander in and out of my inner places. She is the one who listens to my fantasies, sensing in ways she cannot express the differences between me and my siblings.

She makes room for me among old pillows, tugs me through the ragged quilts even as she watches her boys breathe onto the windows. She puts her free arm around me and snuggles Marijo closer, but still she watches her boys. My mother's body blends with her daughters' bodies, holding us close, automatically kissing our hair, sniffing us, but her eyes and intellect are turned toward her boys. She does not look at me again; instead she stares with them toward the fading storm, now turned to a gusty rain. They know the worst is over, but for many long minutes they continue to watch and listen as the lightning moves into the next county, and the rain, less fierce now, threads a steadier pulse into our ears.

But in these moments after a long heat wave, and even as we dread the loss and the work a sudden storm can create, we grow restless with the change of air, the thick green and earth scents. My mother gets up, carries Marijo down the stairs. Then, as though all three of us heard the same call, we look at each other. Suddenly we are racing down the stairs through the dim rooms, spilling onto the back porch, where the rain runs in a silver sheet off the roof. Tom, looking at Rick and me daringly, slips off his pajama bottoms and steps down from the dark wooden steps, naked into the rain, and then, standing in the gravel driveway, he throws his arms out to the sky. To my astonishment, my mother laughs at him, then slips Marijo out of her diaper and lets her run, her small brown legs plowing into the mud of the driveway. Rick, giddy with my mother's permissiveness, strips and runs. Finally, with a nod from her, I step onto the land that is my home, onto the wet earth, into summer rain.

And then we are all out, four naked children running up and down the long yard and into puddles, shaking heavy branches of water over each other, running through the warm rain, over a space as wide and cool and open as the universe, through hills that never end, vistas of blue-green swamp, fine woods, and always over the palm of the great, muddy, living and dying fields.

Apple Gifts

This room, the big attic at the east end of the second floor in the worn old farmhouse, possesses two uncurtained dormer windows that face north, like wide-open but half-blind eyes. Though they invite light, it comes in sideways, the way we learn. The room smells of wool, quilts, trunks, mothballs, and the oily scent of old army uniforms. But most of all it smells like the apples we store there from October to March, individually wrapped in sheets of newspaper and stacked neatly in the bushel crates, tucked into the coolest corner, away from light. If you unwrap one, apple air floats into your face; the room is old and dark, yet unwrapping an apple here is like opening a flower or a present.

Even though the apples are picked in fall and eaten in winter, these seasons are not connected to me; they float without anchors in oatmeal days, thick with a child's untime. When, through a golden September and October, we picked apples in the wind-churned orchards, I did not notice the changes. The windfalls turned into sauce on the stove; tart crab apples were pickled in scarlet syrup. I knew we were putting by but I did not know the more subtle thing, that this was a way of marking time.

My mother sets aside the best apples. These we polish and wrap, hiding them in layers of dry newspaper. My mother treasures them into crates and sets them, as though sacred, into the attic. I never think of them again until the first snows. Through Advent we eat apples instead of ice cream as part of "giving up" things. In January, with a brisk warning not to drop them, we are sent up to carry them down like eggs. All through winter, each time I unwrap one, watching the red skin open against the yellowed paper, I know great security. The apples, small sweet planets, always look the same, lacking the confused ache that has begun to gnaw at me whenever I look closely at myself in the mirror.

Once, during early Lent, having again given up ice cream, I am sent for apples. I creep into the room as though it is a sanctuary and thread my way through a garden of hanging closets and stacked boxes. The cold windows throw down the dormer light, like a glance you aren't supposed to see. Arms loaded, I turn to go and see, tucked against the eaves and caught in the angled light, the rows of old trunks, the uniforms, the quaint dresses drooping their dusty beads like tiny dark insects. I sit down, watching them as though they might move. I smell dust on the bundles in my arms.

I picked apples in October in an orchard of flying leaves. Now the Advent candles have burned to nubs; precious Valentine cards have been forgotten. I unwrap an apple. Its skin has shriveled; the apples are old. I shiver and take a bite. The skin is bitter, textured with age. The pith is still sweet enough, but changed. The room's eyes become mine. I see, half blindly, how it all works, how things move in seasons, sliding sideways through the long winter toward those days that mark time against a different winter.

First Gods

I met the deer in a rye field, a likely home for gods. In summer, after rye seed heads form but before ripening weighs them down, rye stalks are as tall as a ten-year-old child. The dense grain fills the air with lush mint and green so tangible that my siblings and I become euphoric. Summer-free and wild, we do not walk but swim through the waving grain. We thread our way deep into these acres, forming narrow winding paths.

"Here's a good spot," I shout, and we lie down together, rolling, pressing stalks to earth, breaking stems at the surface. We make rooms of broken rye, stems running in one direction like weeds flowing in creek bottoms. We shape walls by leaving a sharp edge of standing rye. These rooms lead to more rooms, linked by halls of broken stems. "This is the living room," I claim. My brothers, disgusted, crawl away to rooms where they can gather makeshift weapons and remember practicality.

"This one's the bathroom," Tom says, leaping up two dozen feet away. His face takes on a look of patient concentration as he pees. We laugh, thrilled at his daring.

We love our rooms because they are secret and forbidden. "Don't tell," Rick whispers. "We'll get in trouble." He's right. Where we have created this place of twisting, roofless tunnels, turns and corners that no human architecture could build, the rye will never grow again. Our father has explained that rye stalks, once broken, die. The field becomes a forbidden Eden.

But my pleasure is stronger than my fear of our father or punishment. My brothers do not return, but I go back day after day. I lie down in the rye rooms, waving green stems like scepters, touching my feet, knees, mouth—drowsing, smelling—feeling abundantly, enchantingly but unconsciously lonely under the square of clear sky.

One hot, midsummer morning, heavy haze blurs the horizon. Stepping into the halls of broken stems, I lope through thick air. When I stand on my toes, I am just tall enough to see across the expanse of drifting seed heads that blur like strands of hair. I move deep into the field, breathing heavily, making new trails, thinking of a more secret room, a green treasure place at the end of a maze.

I don't know how the deer came to be there, but when I see them, everything stops. I stare across the grain at their fine-boned heads and slim necks. I see them scent the air above the seed heads, staring back at me with dark eyes. The two does and a beautifully built spike-horn buck seem disembodied, floating. The buck's fine ruff curves down his throat and neck, mixing with the surface of rye as though he grows from it, some bust lifted from the seed heads, a velvet-spiked flower rising from the tips of new grain. All three seem to hover—bodiless, frightening, and godlike.

We watch each other. They are still; I am still. The light fills with heat and my own wonder. We are caught in this state of grace until the wind rises. My scent swings toward them. The buck twitches his tail and one ear, throws his head. The deer leap away, white tails pluming as their bodies launch through the haze. The sky turns golden as I watch the empty place they have left in the landscape. I am alone again, but now I feel what alone means.

Though I have no words for the experience, I long for their acute attention, that connection. In their utter focus, I feel blessed and linked to them. Isn't this what the great stories tell? Shouldn't I feel this way before a god? In that moment of attention, without any further demonstration, I know I will do anything for them.

I look around. The rye room seems shabby to me, not good enough for the deer. I wander for hours, looking for a place to build a new room, but nothing is worthy. Finally I leave, full of restless desire. I go back many times that summer but I never see the deer again, and I am never satisfied. The next year, when I walk into the field, I have grown taller, and because I can see farther, to the edges of the field and beyond, the rye loses its mystery. But longing holds. Even today, I never see deer on the road, in fields, even hanging from the hunter's tree, without hoping they will look at me inclusively again.

The Barn

Barns place the farmer squarely in the middle of dirt, animals, and reverence. Barns are where things die openly but not serenely: stillborn calves, drowned swallows, frost-bitten kittens. Our barn is a place of largesse and work, open mows and high arching spaces. They are the cathedrals of farms, where all the great rituals are housed.

On days when we can leave the fields and play, Tom and I dare each other to walk the high crossbeams, balancing on the old cross-cut, ax-hewn ten-by-tens.

The first time I hesitate, and Tom taunts me. "Hey you, you're gonna get stuck up there, and somebody'll have to come getcha."

"Yeah, scaredy-cat, fraidy, can't walk the high beam," Rick joins him.

And then I remember what my mother, who is afraid of heights, has said: "Don't look down." I look directly at the beam, at the ladder brace in the middle, and take tentative, wobbly steps all the way across the high beam.

When I am good enough to climb like a cat, I curl onto the ladder and laugh down at my little sisters. Though I am too young to know the words to describe the experience, I love sending dust and pigeon droppings down into the shafts of light. I take pleasure in the way my stomach feels if I nearly lose my balance. Walking that ten-inch-wide beam across the open bays has nothing to do with death, only with the thrill of risk. Walking the crossbeam is a chosen dare. Though my brothers and I say to each other, "You could fall and die," what we mean is "You could fall and hurt yourself." We do not believe ourselves immortal, as teenagers do; we haven't thought of death yet at all.

One day my foster brother, Bobby Barnes, who lives with us while he finishes high school, holds a heavy work rope in his young hands. The rope is winched to an iron eye at the very peak of the barn. Bobby is tall and lanky, with dark brown hair, and in a way that I don't yet understand I like him. He is from a downstate city, Muskegon. He is much older than the other children who sometimes stay with us, and he works long hours with my father. He often plays with me, and he is willing to teach me things. On this day he is teaching me to swing the bay.

The rope hangs and drops loosely down into the center of the bay, that open space where we pull the wagons to unload the hay. Bobby and I take turns hauling the rope up into the north mow. We wrap our legs around it, grab it with our dirty hands, and leap off the high-stacked bales. We swing wildly across the bay to the other side, dropping into the softer, lower mow on the south. The trick is to let go at the right time, before the rope starts its pendulum swing back. And because we are swinging from a high place, the rope, even at the lowest point of its arc, is many feet above the floor of the barn. But we never think of falling, only of the wild swinging and the shrieking as we land in the softer, lower hay on the other side.

Even though I am clumsy, the swing through the dusty air is pure addiction. Bobby does it better than I do. Swinging farther and farther out, he whoops and waves. It becomes a dare, him swinging, then me swinging, seeing if I can fly as high, as far as he can before dropping off onto the other side.

Though I am tired and sweating, I grab the rope. "I want to go higher. Higher than you." I am full of bravado.

"You probably can. You're lighter." He grins. For him the competition is no issue.

This time I twist the rope twice around my foot. This time, as I pull the rope up and back tightly onto the mow, he grabs my hips and lifts me higher, so I can leap from a greater distance. Then he lets go, and I lean back and fly. I slip into the air like a fish, swinging fast, the dusty speed cooling my face. But way out, somewhere in the space between one mow and another, leaning too far back into the slim beams of light, my hands come loose, slipping in their own grime and sweat. Because my feet are wrapped in the rope, the trunk of my body falls first, my ankles untangling last. From several feet in the air, I free-fall, landing on the floor of the barn on my back.

I feel no impact. I know where I am. Staring up through the dust motes in the sprawl of light, I experience a sense of floating, as though I have gained the weightlessness of being under water. And then, in that dim way awareness returns when one is stunned, I realize that I cannot breathe. I cannot breathe. My body tightens. I feel pain in my chest so foreign that a streak of panic rushes through me like nothing I have known in my life. *I cannot breathe.*

I know that I have died.

This sense of not being able to inhale is fiery and alien. No other awareness enters my small intellect. I thrash and roll on the floor, then somehow I stand. Without knowing how or where, I am running, trying to scream, unable to scream.

Somewhere between the barn and the house, I do inhale and scream. The screams bring my mother from the clothesline. Through some wild buzz in my body I see her running too, wiping her hands on the faded apron. In her brown saddle shoes, she clomps down the sunny driveway. She moves closer and closer to me in an odd silence that is also a huge noise in my head, covering the sound of her thudding steps. I do not remember entering her arms. I am simply there, screaming strange, incongruous utterances over and over.

As sense pulls me back into the world, I look down at my chest. My hands are spread across it like wings, as though something in it would break open and escape from my body. I hear my breath at last, rasping but real. I say the words again, more softly, winding down: "I died. I died."

And for every time I say the words, I hear her soft chant, a methodical response to my claim. She is kneeling in the sand on the edge of the barnyard, rocking me, answering over and over, every time. Each time I say "I died," she responds "You're not dead."

I begin to believe her.

But if I am not dead, what was that?

In half-sobbed nonsense, I try to say how we were swinging, how I have fallen. I mutter. My words wind down like a mechanical toy. How can I tell her? I know enough about death to know that breathing is life. If I couldn't breathe, I must have been dead.

"You got the wind knocked out of you." She pulls away and looks into my face.

"The wind knocked out of me?" I am trembling.

"When you fell and hit the barn floor, it knocked all the air out of your chest. It takes a minute for it to come back." She nods.

The wind knocked out of me! Breathing, like wind in a tree, can leave the body and go away and then come back? Is this true? I stare at her for so long that she must look away.

Together, we walk back to the barn. It is still calm and huge, but I am changed. I point tenderly to the rope but do not touch it. I show her where I fell. She explains what happened, the rudiments of a person's lungs. Bobby joins us; he is shy and worried until he realizes that she does not blame him. She says she is glad I am not hurt, asks him not to play this game with me anymore. She walks us back to the house, where she pours Kool-Aid and tells us to find something more constructive to do. My chest and my back hurt, but I know my body is not seriously hurt. However, there is this other awareness, and I am just old enough to think about it.

The awareness comes to rest in the words, the abrupt phrase, *knocked the wind out of you*. I say the phrase over and over. It comes to represent a moment so formative it is forever associated with the thick part of me where breathing is housed. The words and their meaning are linked now in cellular knowing. On that day my mother named for me something that was so like death it negated coming back to the innocence of mere risk. I never again walked the crossbeams or swung on the rope because, with a child's commitment to knowing, I understood that I could die.

The Second Fall

The horse dies in the field where the artesian well flows. This spring shoots water out of the ground like a hose under pressure, and we call it the "flowing well." Before that day the horse lived in this field, drank from the livestock tank filled by the well, and grazed on the rich grasses and bluestem growing along the banks of the stream formed by the well. They called the horse Mike. Now his bloated body, round and stretched wide, legs stuck in the air like giant pencils, is too huge to move. My Uncle Butler, who owns Mike, calls the local fire chief to ask permission to burn the carcass. The man says, "Do what you gotta do."

My father and Uncle Butler cover this huge mound of animal with brush and gasoline. When they light it, the smoke rolls so high and dark that neighbors find their way to the field, step out of their old Buicks and Fords, and stand around with their arms crossed, watching him burn. "Big horse," they agree, their craggy faces nodding at the fire. They watch the way people who know animal death watch, curious but detached from years of exposure.

At one point the fire creates an odd silhouette, the brush burning more brightly on the far side than on the near side. I see the shape of the animal through flames; its bloated shape reminds me of something pregnant. Gratefully, I watch the horse burn.

Uncle Butler, who lives in the farmhouse a quarter mile to the north, raises horses. We are as excited as small birds by these creatures of hide and strength. We visit them in the warm evenings when the sky is finally cool. We touch their moss-soft noses, listen to their guttural horse language, always from the depths of their throats. We adoringly offer them carrots and stolen apples.

I am still less than ten when my uncle purchases this biggest horse, this dark monster of a horse. It is his greatest prize, and each of us is expected to be deeply honored to take a turn riding it.

On a Sunday evening we gather in my uncle's yard, at the edge of the rough corral. The boys take turns riding slowly around the house, up the hill, and back. Though I too love horses, it is simply because they are animals. I am not intuitive about horses, not a natural rider. I do not understand their strength. I am curious about riding them, but never comfortable. And this creature seems bigger to me than anything I have known, certainly bigger than the cows, bigger than the bull. I watch it throw its head up and yank the leather straps out of my dad's hands. The men use their soft voices to keep it from dancing. Still it prances, side-steps, lifting its feet up and down unpredictably.

My uncle turns to me, winking, "It's your turn now. Those boys have had enough time on the beast."

"Hey girl, let's get you up there." My father slaps his thigh and reaches for me.

"I don't want to ride today."

"Sure you do. You been talking about it all week." Before I have time to stop him, I feel his strong arms under my own. When I am boosted onto the saddle and settle into the seat of the leather, I know I am too high. I grab onto the saddle horn and hunch over the dark neck of the horse, biting my lips, wordless.

"Hey, OK?" my Uncle Butler asks. I am not, but in the face of his optimism, I nod a little.

"Not afraid, are you?" my dad asks. I look at my brothers, watching me.

"Uh-huh."

"You'll be just fine," says Uncle Butler, prying my hands from the saddle horn.

"You can't hold the saddle horn," my father tells me.

I grab the mane.

"Not there either. You gotta take the reins."

They force the reins into my hands.

"Squeeze with your knees." Then Uncle Butler tells me all I have to do is tug the reins and the horse will stop. It's halter trained. They remind me of words I know: *Giddup* and *Whoa*, the words of riding. They let go of me and the horse. I try to tell them that this horse is different from the others. They laugh, saying *Yup, he is*. I try to tell them I don't want to ride today. They do not believe me.

The horse stands on the flat yard bordered by a rise to the house. He takes a few steps forward, stops, then begins to walk again, the thud of his hooves dull in the grass. After a few yards he begins to sidle sideways up the slope, off the safe, familiar ground. The men and my little brothers have turned away, talking under a tree.

Mike stops again, tosses his boulder-like head wildly. I grab the pommel, tangling the reins. I'm not quite tall enough to bear down on the stirrups, and his movement up the slope throws me off balance. Everything feels too high. He walks again, up the yard. I shift a little, trying to keep my seat. He sidesteps and moves a little faster. I slip more. He dances, lifting his hooves up and down, punctuating his rhythm of power. Slowly, without fanfare, pulling the reins, I slide sideways. With only the smallest thunk, I fall off, crumpling on the ground like an empty sack.

Though the heels of my hands are scraped and my knees ache, I am not hurt by this fall. I do not cry out when I roll over and see the horse standing above me. He snorts. My body jerks in reaction. I am a small rodent that surprises him. I see the horse's head above me, huge and restless, his large black eyes staring down at me. It is as though he can read my mind, and I know, in that place where children have extra senses, that the horse knows I am afraid.

I let them put me back on.

"It's nothing, nothing scary at all," Uncle Butler says, after he has picked me up and dusted me off, chuckling as though this ride is a bright Sunday. He heaves me up and back into the saddle. This time they walk beside me, reciting the rule, "You got to get right back on. You got to do that or you'll never get on again." I know they believe these things, so I let them hoist me back up. I hear my father's voice encouraging me. My uncle, leading a now perfectly docile animal, talks rousingly of how horses have thrown him. This was not a throw. I know that. This was something smaller and less important, and it should not have frightened me. They make me ride, walking beside me until I stop crying. It does not take long because I know the ride will not end until they are convinced I am fearless.

"You OK now?" my father asks.

"Can I get down?"

"Sure. See? Nothing to be afraid of."

I nod. My brothers giggle. From this day on, even though I had gotten right back on, just as they asked, I will never ride this horse again. They think I have overcome fear. I have not. I stop crying because, for the first time, I am too furious for tears. They refuse to believe me. They are not listening to me. And they will not listen. They see their way, not mine. They are choosing my lessons, but for the first time I see that my way does exist, a narrow but real refusal to ride the biggest horse.

The day before they burn Mike, lightning came down in that broad, spring-fed field and "Struck 'im dead," my Uncle Butler says. Until then, I believed that lightning only struck trees, barns, houses, never living things. To me, the fact that lightning should strike this massive animal feels right, like the justice of the Bible stories I have begun to read.

When my brothers and I hear the news, we hit the road like dogs on a scent, following the gravel track to those wide pastured acres where the frigid creek runs through cropped grasses. We talk all the way about the lightning, the storm, the wild sounds, and the phenomenal event: a horse killed by lightning.

We stop before the carcass, silenced.

"Wow." My brothers make noises that are not words. They whistle. "Look at him. He's really dead." They walk around him, poking the carcass with sticks, daring each other to touch him. They look for the hole they think the bolt of lightning burned through him and are disappointed not to find even a seared edge, though the hide is darker than it should be.

I wonder why he doesn't get up. I expect to see him rise in that clumsy way that horses have of lifting themselves from their sleeping places. Why doesn't he get up, shake the dirt off his hide and mane, and gallop across the field, nickering gruffly. I think his mouth should be closed. I begin to see the distortion this death is making, the stink and nothingness in the open mouth full of black tongue and flies. I smell him, only part horse now and mostly death. I see that he is swelling, taking on the hugeness of decay. Then I look into his flat eyes. I have learned something of how eyes work, how they change. I can sometimes read them better than words. I know for sure he is not going to get up. I know now what the change I felt inside looks like on the outside, looks like in grass and dirt and yesterday's rain.

I am glad they will burn him. I am glad I will never have to look at this animal again. I am glad he is dead. I turn away and run toward the well, toward the lush grass around the flowing water. I climb into the stock tank and sit there, soaking in the chill water.

My brothers are sure I am crazy.

Much later, the summer I am thirteen, I think I understand. Before I leave the farm to become another person, I work in that field where Mike was struck by lightning. I am sorting tart cherries into big tanks at the flowing well. The water explodes through a new fitting and shapes an ice-cold stream. The snout of the hose bubbles into the large metal cherry tanks and spills over into the quiet pasture. The cherries are stored in the tanks until they are loaded onto the flatbed semi and hauled to the processor.

My fingers are blue and stiff, but I sluice leaves, blossom heads, and pesticide slick from the surface water onto the muddy, wild grass. I am soaked from my abdomen to my ankles. I run a screen deep into the tanks, stirring the cherries, filtering them through my fingers, looking for fruit bruised by winds or birds. On the ground near my feet is a lug of marred cherries. These will be used for juice. "Can't go to waste," my mother will say when we crush them.

I take off my damp shirt so the July sun hits my back. I am so cold I don't care who might see me. I realize it will be an hour before the next tank is full. Then my dad or one of my brothers will come with the fork-lift, wobbling down the road with a new tank perched on the heavy tines of the lift. I slosh the cold water. I am trying to find some fantasy big enough to take my mind away from the cold water for a while. This is a trick I have learned so that I can keep working.

I look up, over the sunny field. I remember the big horse, his massive size, his huge feet. I remember looking up at his huge face and his underbelly strapped in leather. Something must remain.

I walk away from the tanks, crossing the field, shuffling in the weeds, stumbling over the long grasses. I begin to look more purposefully, kicking through wild vetch, looking for a charred spot, a place where the weeds are stunted. I comb my hands through bluestem and brome grass, breaking Queen Anne's Lace and milkweed.

He is gone.

This animal's remains have disappeared. I stand still. I know the day he threw me, the day he died, and the day we burned him. But this horse, the biggest horse in my world, the creature who, even in his death, seemed larger than life, is invisible because the lush growth from an artesian well has returned that land to itself. There is nothing here but this wild field. Not a bone.

My hands, warming up, hurt. I walk back through the grasses to the tanks, pull on my shirt, and plunge my hands into the water. I tell myself that my brothers could walk to the place, could kick the dirt and turn up a chip, an iron shoe. But I cannot find it. I tell myself I will ask them. After they show me, I will place a stone to mark it. I never do.

I pick and sort and sluice. In the bright July sun, I am shivering. I keep my hands in the water. I save the bruised cherries for juice. As it has for years, the cold, prophetic water rushes out of the earth.

Killdeer

Asparagus is the first of the spring harvests. Frenzied by the heat of May and June, asparagus fields may be ready to pick twice a day. And when asparagus is ready, farmers pick. That means their children pick. Depending on the year, three or four or five of us rise at six and head out to the fields. As we start off, we read the thermometer nailed to the outside of the workshop. There are heat waves, even in Michigan—even that close to Lake Michigan—that soar into the nineties. We pick through this heat until dark. We pick every summer from the time we are seven years old.

Even here, in these gray fields, respites exist. Killdeer, birds with bibs and collars and trim black-and-white wing bands, always look cool. And each year, somewhere in the fields, three or four pairs of killdeer build crude nests and lay spotted, perfectly camouflaged eggs. With each sweep down the rows, the workers come nearer to the nests. Progressively, the killdeer calls more quickly. As it becomes obvious that people are endangering the nest, the bird, driven to panic, plays a deceptive game. It pretends to have a broken wing. It crawls quickly away from the nest, dragging its beautiful bands in a splay of black and white. Its cry changes, becoming more frantic, darker, shriller, wounded. The bird begs you to come after it, claiming it is easy prey. Its dance says, *You may have this broken carcass for the asking; you may simply pick me up from the dust and I will be your meat.*

If you follow it, the bird will stutter its wings in the dust. Pretending a violent wound but moving quickly, it will pull itself farther from the nest, leading you away from the spotted eggs. You will follow as though the bird were a piper. The bird teases you away, tugging at your eyes like a skilled actress, seducing you with her language. Your steps follow the scrape of wings in the dust. You know you can touch her. When you are thoroughly wrapped in this siren's act, the bird becomes well again and takes off, winding its cry in a screech of triumph. It will circle away from you, and, if you do not turn back, it will return to the nest, settling like water on the gray sticks, rounded gravel, and spotted eggs.

The problem is with the rider, an iron and wood platform—also called a picker—with wheels at each end, on which the workers sit. This cannot be turned away. It cannot be distracted. It *must* follow the rows. Even if the driver sees the delicate bird, he does not, cannot turn aside from the rows for fear of crushing the thin green stems of the asparagus crop. Most riders sprawl over five or seven rows, with a crew member riding each row, legs spread to footholds on each side of a rough seat that perches six inches above the ground. We pick the spears by hand as the row, like a stony treadmill, moves under our seats.

This machine is dragged for hours over hot acres. With each round, up and down the rows, we come closer to the nest. We watch the bird, alert to us, increase its cries of warning, then its nervous movement. Finally, as the inevitable becomes real, the bird assumes its broken-wing act directly in front of the rider, within a few inches of the great tractor tires. Fearlessly the bird calls *take me, take me,* and sometimes, with birds whose eggs are about to hatch, they dart close to our hands. Unable to resist, we reach for feathers instead of green stalks. If we are very lucky, we can stroke cool feathers before the bird slips away from our fingers, leaving a ghost of air.

We begin to watch for the nest. Usually killdeer make their nests in the middle of the row, where the rough soil hides the nest. We consider it lucky to ride over the row that hides the nest. If we see it, and keep our eyes on it, it is worth risking our father's sharp reprimand to watch the delicate, nearly invisible eggs as they pass under the shadow of the rider. We watch as though hypnotized. If we turn our eyes away even a flicker, we will lose them. If we could explain, we would say our fascination stems from seeing something that so perfectly reflects our own invisibility. In a last tormented scream, the bird, dragging and broken, watches her act revealed as ruse while the shadow of the rider passes over her eggs. The bird, silent in a rough of feathers, knows all is lost. Our shadow consumes its nest. Suddenly aware of its own dangerous situation in front of a John Deere and rider, the bird takes flight.

Even on the hottest days, what happens next is more resurrective than rain. As it circles in despair, there comes a moment, after we have passed over, when it sees its nest again, untouched, eggs intact.

Some birds land silently, uttering no cry of acknowledgment, but most killdeer offer one stiff, brief call of recognition. Then they settle. It is as if we never touched their world. This is a farm again, and we are just farmers. The heat rolls back, and we forget the killdeer's impossible eggs and its fearless, illusory dance against the machine.

Violence

Of the two barns, the smaller one, with a corn shed clinging to its side like a tipsy man leaning on a fence, is older and more battered. It is the barn where dried beans were stored decades before, when the area was called "Beantown." No matter how many times we use it for storing straw, I can always find a few small, white navy beans, their creamy, fragile pods splayed open as if a knife cut them in two. Sometimes I gather them and try to fit the two parts together, try to make them one piece again. I can't, of course, but there is something about collecting a basket of the fragile pods, a manyness I enjoy. I often play in this barn, gathering the pods, which I conceive of as dollars or magic shells or even the parchment of spells.

In that particular barn there are cats. Here we also raise calves, keeping them separate from the cattle in the big barn. It has a low loft, no more than ten feet high, with wooden ladders we scamper up like weasels. Under the loft is the stable where we keep the calves. The cats seem to prefer living with the calves as opposed to the cows, and they nest their litters in the straw in this barn. The litters grow up wild and don't live long before winter or sickness takes them. But I sneak into the barn and call to them, crooning for them to come to me—though they seldom do, unless I bring treats. If they crawl out of their hidden places, they are inclined to roll and play coyly in my lap, then suddenly turn and scratch, becoming wild creatures I do not recognize. Once, after I become particularly attached to one toddling litter, I crawl to their nest in the straw only to discover they are all dead, half chewed, their throats mangled by a muscular tearing bite.

My mother, calming my hysteria, tells me the tomcat killed them.

"Killed them, but why?"

"I don't know; it's something they do sometimes. They get jealous."

"Jealous? What's that mean?"

"When you want something that someone else has got."

"But what do they have?"

"The mother cat spends her time with the kittens now."

"But the tom is the daddy."

My mother is quiet, holding me. "Yes, but in the animal world, he doesn't know that. He only knows that these things make him mad."

"We should kill the tomcat."

"Then there would be no more kittens and a lot more rats."

I think a lot about the kittens, about the *killing* of the kittens, the way it must have been for them to look so torn open. The word I learn later is *ravaged*.

There comes a time when we have no calves or hay in this barn, and for some reason the red, sliding, barn door is locked, its rusty hook set too high for us to reach up and flip open. We climb into the barn through a hole in the foundation, where the rocks have come loose from under the sill timbers, and if we wriggle through the dirt we rise up inside like ferrets into their dens. Because this barn is older, there are more open knots in the old pine siding. When the sun hits the barn these holes create tiny circular beams of light on the floor of the small bay. They spread like dot-to-dot drawings over the scarred wood.

In this barn, in the loft, our father stores old tools and parts of machines and equipment; perhaps this is why the door is locked. We are already notorious for injuring ourselves on nails and the shards of metal that jump loose from equipment and machines everywhere on a farm. But because it is locked, we must go in.

I am a little older and am now sometimes left in charge of the boys, which means I am supposed to keep them out of trouble. They are at the age where they are inseparable and nearly the same height. Though the shape of their noses is different—one narrow, one wide—they have the same pale hair and gray eyes, wide faces, the same full mouths that mark our family. They move in wild tandems. They run apart, then together, then apart—but never very far apart—and often they both run away at the same time without either of them suggesting it, as though the thought came to them at the same time. Alone together, they fish in the stocked ponds down the road or build fantastic frog reservoirs in the creeks. After my mother calls and calls and frantically rings the dinner bell, she sometimes walks out into the fields, to the gravel pit perhaps, where she sees their faces rise together like small snuffling animals, side by side, alert, attentive. They return to their work without acknowledging her. Their own activities and ideas sustain them, and they rarely seem to need anyone. They are always called *the boys*.

We are playing in the loft over the stable. It is a child's gold mine, filled with pieces of barrel staves and the circular iron bindings that hold them, as well as parts of the old irrigation system, the clamps used to hold the pipes together, a broken hammer, two gray squirrel tails, bird feathers, pigeon droppings.

Tom looks down over the edge of the loft into the bay. He has a body that feels alive and willing to do anything. He runs to the edge of the loft and stops, pretending to wave wildly, catching his balance.

"Cut it out," I tell him, but he does it again, giggling wildly.

He scampers down the ladder and looks up at us. "Hey, it's not that high. I can jump." He scrambles back up, but when he gets up to the top again he feels the height and hesitates. He is not foolish; his survival instincts are in place. But he already enjoys defying the world he encounters. He is a critical year older than Rick, and though it rarely matters, he can sometimes judge distances better.

He flops down on his stomach at the edge of the loft. Rick crawls down with him, and they both reach as far as they can over the edge, their fingers groping for some reassurance that this ledge is not as high as they think it is.

"It's pretty high," Rick says.

"Not that high."

"Pretty high to jump."

I pick up my bucket of pods and dried beans, the treasures I wish to keep, and start down the ladder, balancing the metal pail in the crook of one elbow. "Come on, boys, let's go."

"Why?" They look at me in disbelief.

"Because no one is going to jump. You'll get hurt. And we're not even supposed to be here."

They stare at each other. They want to jump like they want food. I can see it in the way both mouths set, but for the first time neither is quite prepared to go first. Some bigger thing will have to push them to the jump. I call again, trying to bring up from my throat the authority my mother has.

"Come down right now or I'm going to tell Mom on you."

They are only momentarily nonplused. Then my authority becomes the trigger for their defiance. Tom turns to Rick. "Before she tells, I dare you to jump."

What is it about the word *dare*?

They look down together. They are so much a part of each other. They turn their heads together, looking down the west wall and then back east, looking for one place that might be lower, less rickety than another. Rick gets up and paces back and forth along the dusty edge. I can see he feels trapped by the dare. He has that squashed look on his face that he gets when he can't do something he wants to. Tom is smiling. Rick turns, catches it, and his face turns red. What he says next surprises Tom. "I dare *you.*"

It is like a sheet of paper being torn in half.

Tom's face changes, "You can't dare me."

"Why not?"

"I dared you first."

"So. You can't dare me back until you do the dare."

Tom looks at him. Then slowly, in a voice I have never heard before, "I double dog dare you."

This is too much. Rick assumes the face of a nocturnal animal looking at a too-bright light. The dots of light shift on the floor. The kitten I have been trying to lure from a nest hurtles back into its small tunnel. I call up to them, "Hey, no one gets to dare anyone."

They look at each other again, shaky and closed.

"I said, you can't dare or double dog dare." I'm standing now, the bucket and kitten forgotten. "Let's get out of here."

Tom begins the chant, "I double dog, double dog, double dog dare you."

"There's no such thing," I holler.

Rick turns like a string puppet being manipulated by an amateur. He backs up a few steps, takes a running start, and with his small legs still whirring in the air runs off the edge of the loft. He passes through the beams of light. He hits the floor and falls on his knees, crying out as he rolls to the side, almost somersaulting in the dust. He lays still for a moment, holding his knees. Then he gets up. He looks up at the loft where Tom is looking down.

"I dare you to jump," Rick says, his voice fierce and dog-like in his small body.

Tom's face is bright again. He looks down. It is his turn to pace.

Until now, I have seen my brothers as one, matched in every way, but I know from their checker games that Tom is not an easy loser; he often wins at the last minute with a turn of the rules. I try again. "You boys, stop. Tom, come down from there or I'm going to get Mom right now," I am awed that Rick has jumped, but I cannot let him know. I think maybe they will let it go now.

But Rick will not let it go. "Go get her." He is full of his triumph and will not even touch the frayed knees of his jeans where the welts rise. Then, looking up at his brother, he says, "I double dog, double dog, double dog dare you."

Tom has moved back into the loft. I can hear him bumping in the back hollow places. He rummages among the junk and broken things, clanging and dragging. He comes back with a long pole. He drops it down the wall but keeps hold of one end. It does not touch the floor. He pulls it up and looks at it and knows he will fall farther than that distance. He looks down. Rick grows restless. In a new voice, he begins the singsong taunt that will spur his brother's temper.

"Scaredy-cat, scaredy-cat, scaredy-cat . . . ," and he moves across the boards, swinging his arms, stepping in and out among the dots of light in a kind of dance for which there are no steps.

"I'm not scared," Tom shouts down, breathing hard.

"Scaredy-cat, just a big ole scaredy-cat."

"Rick, stop it." I try to touch him, but Rick is not to be touched on this day. "Tom, come on down." I turn to him, but he begins to rock back and forth, captured in a new territory.

Tom rocks and swings his head from side to side. He is not crying, but I think that if he would, then I could get him to come down. Rick speeds up the chant, "Scaredy, scaredy, quite contrary, how does your garden grow?"

"Don't call me scaredy," Tom says.

Rick does not stop. *Scaredy, scaredy.*

"If you stop singing that, I'll jump," Tom announces.

I hold my breath.

Rick laughs and repeats, "Scaredy-cat, scaredy-cat. . . ."

Tom turns his back and walks away from the lip of the loft, look-ing for something. We hear him trot back to the pile of machinery. When his body appears again at the edge of the loft, he is lugging a metallic cylinder riddled with wires and casings with strange holes and grids wrapping a copper core. It is a small but heavy motor, its innards half revealed and coiled. Tom walks awkwardly, as though he were carrying something dead. He looks down at Rick. "You shut up," he says. "You shut up or I'm going to hit you with this."

Rick looks up, continues the chant, turning it into a distorted song. The only words are "scaredy-cat" in high pitches and low pitches, like the tones of a Halloween monster. The words move like a hunting cat, melodic then abrupt. I have never heard him do this before, but I recog-nize that this is something I do. I am hearing the moment from the out-side for the first time, when words become simply sound. I realize Rick has forgotten the meaning of these words, that he is looking at but not listening to Tom. He is hearing the refrain of raw and repeated sound in his head, "Scaredy, scaredy, scaredy-cat."

Tom does not see what I see. He is wrapped in a green anger as he shouts down, more loudly and shrilly, "You stop or I'm gonna kill you."

He lifts the motor, staggering under its weight, until it is above his head.

"Tom, put it down. Please, put it down." I am begging.

"*Scaredy, scaredy, scaredy-cat.*"

Tom lifts it in his arms and throws it over the edge of the loft. The dark metal object falls with a directness that lacks the curve of things that are tossed. It falls, not like a baseball or even a stone. It plummets, a straight answer to gravity. Rick sees it too, and he knows the aim is true, and he moves but not fast enough.

I see only that it hits his head as it drops, and he falls hard, as though a huge hand slapped his whole body down. His hands cover his head and he screams. Blood leaks between his fingers, down his arms, dripping onto the floor. I look up at Tom. His mouth is open, a thin searing sound coming from it. This is the mouth of a little boy who has entered a place he cannot leave. He is on his knees and his face is streaming. "I told him to stop, told him to stop, told him."

I turn and stumble through the broken straw, through the dusty light, and throw myself, wiggling and gasping through the hole in the foundation. I come up into ordinary daylight, light without drama, and the screams inside become muted. The breeze from the south kicks the scent of manure into the air. The sun is bright. Up the slope in the back yard, laundry flaps; the windmill creaks. I remember the blood and keep running, calling now for my mother, announcing to her, announcing the one thing I am sure of in that moment: "Tom killed Rick. Tom killed Rick."

Why that word? *Killed?*

Tom had not killed Rick. By the time my mother reached them, Tom was using his tee-shirt to sop the blood, and they were fabricating the lies that would keep them both out of trouble. They were scolded; I was scolded. Rick developed a signature scar on his forehead which he proudly announced to the neighbors that his brother did for him. *For him.* Neither of them talk about the moment after Tom dropped the motor and it hit Rick's head. Neither of them ever brings up why it happened.

I go to the barn again and again. I try to match pods, but they will never fit. I think about what the falling motor looked like, replaying that moment of impact. And I imagine and reimagine the moment the big male cat pounced on the kittens in the litter and opened their throats, ravaging their innocence and taking back by any means necessary the power it once had.

Winter Fields

The temperature in the old farmhouse varies directly with the cold outside. Even the newly installed coal stoker, which allows us to heat the house all night, cannot fight uninsulated walls and caulking lost from storm windows. If the temperature outside drops below ten, inside the house it drops to sixty-five; below zero, it drops to fifty-five. It steadies and hovers there according to the wind, and we gather around old wrought iron heat registers in layered clothing. When school is canceled because of snow and cold, we five—wild, undisciplined, all under twelve—are bored and bicker about the temperature in dramatic tones.

"Mom said it'll be ten below tonight," I announce.

"Ten below. I bet twenty below," Tom says. He's always bragging.

"Or a hundred," I best him.

"It can't get to be a hundred below," Rick says, looking up from his Tinkertoys.

"Sure it can. At the North Pole, it can get colder than that." I know this for sure.

"Naw it can't."

"I learned it in geography."

Marijo stares intently out the window as Patti, the littlest, stumbles against her.

When the cold deepens, my mother makes soups, but she watches the windows. She scrapes frost from the kitchen panes so she can read the thermometer, and she looks out toward the barns. She calls the dogs into the basement and lures the barn cats into the boot room. In the afternoon she will walk out to feed the rabbits in the old milk house converted to a hutch.

The snow is deceptive because it masks the cold. Living things were not meant to work or even move in these kinds of temperatures. Take a lesson from the fields; close your eyes, think into the darkness of soil and stone. But we move, and things happen. We make mistakes. In this cold, behavior cannot bear any carelessness, and all carelessness, even the smallest error, multiplies, blind and huge in the cold.

Late morning, during a lull in the storm, as snow comes down sweetly for an hour, we bundle up in wool snowsuits, in jackets with layers of sweaters underneath. We race to the nearest hill with our rickety sleds and that chariot of snow machines, our toboggan. A toboggan slides fast over new snow, rides the small moguls in leaps, like a diver. Because it steers badly, danger increases with its speed. We have seen the toboggan's unpredictability, how on a good run it noses out the only barbed wire fence uncovered for a mile, or how it aims for the only tree on a snowy hillside. We have seen it leap a well-groomed run and take off over a wild bluff, dumping riders into the gray depth of drifts. We love it.

That morning the air turns arctic within minutes of our arriving at the hill. Two good runs and our noses whiten with cold, our doubled mittens cannot keep our thumbs from numbing. When we cannot feel our heels or toes, we trudge back to the house with a variety of wet clothes and complaints, disrupting our mother's only quiet minutes in what promises to be a day full of complaints.

Tom, obsessed with the toboggan, wants to change his clothes, put on Dad's big hunting jacket, and go outside again. Mom can see the wind picking up, this time laced with heavy clots of lake-effect snow, and the fields have disappeared into their white dreams. *No, you can't go out.*

Peanut butter and jelly sandwiches with potato soup and saltines do not improve our mood. We argue about Dad, working at a factory this winter in a town downstate, and whether he will get home through fifteen miles of drifted back roads; we argue about the checker game, the Lincoln Logs, who should play in the tent under the card table. We irritate each other by shouting, "Plow's coming"—a signal to race to the window and lean against the glass, looking as far north or south as vision will permit. Then the perpetrator yells, "April Fool" (no matter it is mid-February), and we all yell back in disappointment. After being tricked twice, I ask Mom if the plows will ever come through. "I doubt it, not today. Not until it lets up."

"Why not?" I don't want to be fooled again.

"I don't think plows will do any good," she says. "It's coming down so hard, the roads would blow in before we can get out and back."

"Do we have enough food?" Tom wants to know.

"Enough for a couple days. All the basic stuff anyway."

This worries us. I wonder if she has anything other than macaroni and cheese or creamed vegetables. I don't think there is a chance she has real hot dogs or canned spaghetti (my personal favorite) tucked away in the pantry.

We love the plows. When the huge orange trucks growl fiercely through a storm, their great engines toiling, they can be heard for miles, and their thunder on a gravel road sends us into spasms of excitement as we watch the great sprays of snow fly up and out and over the banks. We love when the plows stop, pull back, take another run at a deep or stubborn drift. We pride ourselves in living directly across from a northwest field that ends in a small bluff, shaping a six-foot drop into the ditch. Here a good wind could fill the ditch, then blow over the bluff, filling the road until the snow is level all the way across the road, five or six feet deep. Twice this year the plows have gotten stuck there, and when they did break through, they graded ten-foot banks into a series of high, narrow terraces leading up and back like broad stairs to the field.

Tom is watching the road fill again. "We can toboggan on that bank I bet."

"I doubt it." I have a habit of false superiority because I am the oldest.

"Sure you could; look at it," he argues. "You start at the top, then slide over the first bump—it's almost filled in—and then real fast down and 'cross the road."

"That's stupid. You'll kill yourself when you hit bottom. Besides, it's too cold."

But Tom has a clean hold on the idea now.

"Yeah, I can do it . . . ," he breathes softly onto the glass.

Mom is fed up with all of us. She pulls on Dad's big coat. "I'm going to go feed the rabbits. Try not to kill each other while I'm gone."

Tom begs her to let him go with her until finally she says, "All right. Hurry up. And don't forget dry mittens."

When they leave the house, I stare out the kitchen window. I see them trudging across the yard and down the slope to the barely visible barns, Tom trailing the toboggan behind him. The wind screams harder now; I can feel drafts all across the woven rugs that cover the floor. The snow blows at the yard in sheets and wild pivots, and I can barely see the yard light, only fifty feet from the house. When I lean across the kitchen sink and breathe on the window glass, the little red line on the thermometer is so low I cannot find its mark beneath the sill.

I wish they would come back. With Mom and my closest sibling outside in that world, I have no one to fight with.

I see it happening like this.

"Come in when you get cold," she says as she leaves him. She doesn't expect it will be long.

The boy leaves his mother at the edge of the barnyard, and veers off the path, pulling the curved thrum of wood lightly over the top of snow in which he moves like a drunk. He comes to the edge of the road and slips over the bank nearest the barns. He is surprised as he sinks to his hips in the light fluff that has gathered in the trough of winter road. He laughs out loud, runs his mittens over his face with delight, then tugs the twine that leashes the toboggan.

For him, the toboggan is a soaring bird. He dreams of riding its long neck, of fields becoming wide wings as he skims over acres, gaining speed, finally leaping like a great goose from a pond, off the fence rows into the snowy air.

He is sweating by the time he reaches the top of the other bank. As he turns and positions the toboggan, he realizes that his siblings, always clinging to his back on the rides, gave the toboggan weight it doesn't have now. It'll go faster. He sets the toboggan at the brink of the highest point of the bank and curls himself into the front of it, knees tucked under. With his hands in the soft snow, he pushes the toboggan forward. It sticks, and he jerks the trunk of his body forward, thrusting himself farther and farther to the front of the toboggan, balanced at the top edge of the bluff. It begins to teeter, an unwieldy lever on a high, icy fulcrum. Then it tips forward, and finally, as his body leans over the curved wooden lip, it hurtles down the white steepness of the ice and hard-packed snowbank. As it hits the first tier, the toboggan's force slams the boy's body against its lip. It bends and thrums, careens over the second tier, and moves steeply ahead—so steeply that the boy's already off-balance body bounces, loose in a split-second free fall. The toboggan hits the next tier; the small body hurtles onto the curved tooth of wood for a second time, and the boy crumples against it.

After checking two winter nests, our mother knows that they will lose some of the winter litters. The bunnies, too small even in nests insulated with fur from the doe's stomach, will not survive this kind of cold. She sighs, wonders if she could run an extension cord with a space heater, then remembers they have had no power in the barn since the last windstorm. She fills the water and grain troughs, hefting the fifty-pound bags despite the weak back that has plagued her since the last pregnancy. She leaves the milk house and

walks under the eaves of the barn to the big basement area where a few cat-
tle are still housed. She looks in, checks their hay, and heads back across the
barnyard to the house. At the gate she stops. Even through the snow, she
senses that the door of the milk house is open. Not believing she has left it
unlatched, she sighs and tries to talk herself out of it. She gives up and
crosses back to the shed.

The door is open a crack. If she pulls it shut, the latch will fall and
catch. She looks up and checks for the boy who should be visible from here,
playing on the distant bluff, but she does not see him. Probably on the other
side of the bank. She reaches to pull the latch closed when she hears a soft
exhalation over wind, and her chill is suddenly from inside, right at the
belt, where fear rises.

He is lying on the floor of the milk house, curled like a doe around
her litter, with nothing to hold except his own vomit, distinctly laced with
blood. She feels horror so strong that she too feels nauseous. Then her head
clears, and she begins to think. He is barely conscious, groaning softly, but
in a minute, as she checks his pulse and wipes his face, he recognizes her.

"Crashed . . . ," he whispers, then his color changes, and he faints
again. She knows she shouldn't move him, but between his shock and the
cold, she has no choice. Ignoring the scream of back muscles for the second
time that day, she slides her arms under his legs and tosses his body against
her chest. Every step of the agonizing trip to the house she is thinking, plan-
ning, thinking.

I am napping on the register when the kitchen door bursts open, and her
voice, in the kind of command that brooks no rebellion, says coolly,
without emotion, "Rick, Tom's hurt. Take two blankets off your bed and
put them over him." She carries him into her bedroom and comes back,
rummaging under the kitchen sink. I come stumbling in. She hands Rick
a bucket. "Put this next to his head."

"What happened?" I ask.

"Stay out of the way." She races for the phone, but our party line is busy. Marcy's kids are talking to their cousins. She tells them to get off "right now." *What's happening?* My mother is always polite to our neighbors. She puts the phone down, then picks it up, listens, and dials quickly but very precisely, as though she cannot make a mistake. It takes me a minute to realize she is calling the hospital in the nearby town. She is waiting, holding onto the phone with both hands, when she sees me, sees my face streaked with wrinkles from an old pillow.

"Don't cry. We haven't got time," she says firmly.

"I wasn't. . . ." But she doesn't hear me, her attention back to the receiver. I hear snatches of meaning. "How far can you get? Are you sure? No, our plows haven't come through. . . . Jackson Road, that's all? I'll call right back." She hangs up, then dials our neighbor's number, her hand trembling. She stares out the window at the weather, chewing her lip. She whirls and looks at the kitchen clock, back out the window, then speaks. "Ed, Tom's hurt. I need help. I've got to get him out. They think they can get an ambulance to the corner of Jackson Road, but they don't think they can get any further. Can your car get through this?"

More talk, a flurry of progressively more frantic exchanges, another call to the hospital, a third to the road commission. She drops the phone and surges out the back door. I pick up the phone slowly, listening to the cold crackle of the line. I put it carefully back on its black cradle.

Rick comes out, pale as the storm. "He's barfing blood," he says, and picks up Patti, rocking her on his lap. She looks confused and fusses. I stand at the window, rolling the edge of a torn drape in my fingers. I am wondering if I should pray when I hear the low clank and shimmer of a car with tire chains. Uncle Ed's rusty Buick, chains wrapping its old tires, labors up the driveway.

There is no sound quite like the chinking sound made by tire chains. It is a small, skidding power against a storm. Then the sound grows more complicated. Behind Uncle Ed, my Uncle Butler drives an ancient truck with a rickety plow blade. While he plows the driveway, Uncle Ed's slow, teenaged daughter, Judy, climbs out of the Buick. She and my mom talk. My mother is trying to explain what must be done at the house. I think my mother is crying. The cold, even here in the house, has become unbearable.

As I watch, moving from window to window, the sound of a tractor thrums in the distance. I see it coming from the north, a small one (my Uncle Joe's, Jensen's?) up to its wheel covers in drifts but chugging along until it idles grumpily at the end of our rough driveway. It faces my Uncle Butler's plow truck, and the two vehicles churn at each other like half buried insects, fantastic creatures, ready to spin white mud across the cold.

My mother has wrapped Tom in the blankets. She carries him as though he were a huge, empty cocoon. Judy shuffles in and stares out the window, sighing.

The men, dark-hooded intelligences, drive worn machines, fueled by oily engines and badly filtered gasoline. The tractor snorts, chugging as far into the depths as it can, then backs up, runs again. My uncle's plow blade swipes a path wide enough for the car. They back up, then race at the drifts again, pounding snow into ruts. An old truck, an old car, an old tractor tear at the icy drive and begin breaking down the drifts enough so that the car with the boy will not get stuck, will not feel one bump more than necessary. Snow mixes with greasy exhaust.

My mother, now a taut face behind a windshield, holds a sweaty, sick bundle and braces herself against the door, aware of what every shudder and tremble means. Even from the windows, I can see that my uncle is moving the car delicately. Flurries pick up, clotting the air. We can barely see this odd caravan of rescue as it evolves into small dark shapes moving away over whitescape. Within five minutes they crest the western hill and disappear down a road that travels through fields whose surfaces are as wide and empty a oceans.

After the sound of engines slides away, I stand at the big window, shivering and watching wind fill the rutted tracks full of shadows. I barely hear Rick leave and come back, announcing that the toboggan is busted. He says he had to dig it out, that Tom must have fallen against it sliding down the bank. He is awed, admiring the mess his brother has made of the toboggan.

The little girls have cried on and off, huddled together on the living room couch. Judy is sweeping the floor, complaining that she should not have to do our work.

I stare at the smooth fields. I think about my brother, how badly he must be hurt. I wonder if they will make it and, if they do, will it be in time to save him. The wind races off the field and shoves itself in a great bluster against the window. I touch the cold glass. The fields look blind.

I turn from the window. I go to Tom's bedroom and throw myself on his bed. Judy comes in.

"Why you crying?" she asks in her slow voice.

I don't answer, so she pulls me up. "How come yer crying?"

"It's all my fault," I say. Even as I say these words, I know they are not true.

She looks confused, "You didn't hurt him, did you?" Then she says, without smiling, "You need work to do." She puts the dish towel in my hand.

"Is Tom going to die?" I ask, closer to the heart of it.

"Nobody said anything about it," she says, and tugs me back to the kitchen where the dishes are already draining.

My brother broke two ribs, but one of the ribs ruptured his spleen. That small caravan took an hour to move him fifteen miles into town. Doctors, slowed by the storm, took another hour to begin the surgery to remove his spleen. The internal bleeding continued. My father finally arrived from Du Pont, joining my frantic mother. They were told that

Tom's chances were slim. That night, my mother and father, embarrassed to pray the rosary in public, sat in their car in the hospital parking lot, turning the engine on and off to keep warm, whispering Hail Marys back and forth to each other. The priest gave my brother the last rites.

Twenty-four hours later he was still alive, weak but conscious. Forty-eight hours after that he sneaked out of bed, stole a wheelchair, and raced several geriatric patients down the hall before he was caught and led sternly back to bed. His fever receded and then inexplicably rose, high enough to assume infection. A day later he broke out in spots. Chicken pox. He'd been exposed at school, and in the next two weeks, like clockwork, the rest of us all broke out in spots.

But in my memory I dry dishes and pick up toys and look out the windows of a cold house. I look out at the fields and begin to feel how far away they are, eyeing them with—a word I do not yet have— *detachment*. I look without peace, with only this new knowledge: that the storm and these white fields do not care for my brother or me, that we cannot touch or change the fields.

Weather Changes

I sleep—against the protests of my younger brothers—in the big upstairs room with three west windows that look out through high branches of the silver maple. From those windows, I watch the sun go down and the weather move in. In winter the glass rattles because the caulking is gone. It frosts up in wild, splayed patterns because there are no storm windows. On a clear summer day the view from these windows tells me about the weather changes in the night. I say my prayers looking out those windows. *Now I lay me down to sleep. . . .* Then I climb into the big, wide bed with the battered headboard, down under the Aunt Mary quilts and into the plain cotton sheets that are always cold. Rolling onto my left side, I watch the shadows of the great tree, the distant yard light at Smith's farm, and the faraway lights of some remote world on the horizon.

My father is afraid of windstorms.

When I wake up, the thunder is a damp, angry thing with heavy wings, and the room is flashing with green light. The big tree in the front yard holds up a thousand arms, all waving east. The moist wind, banging against the screen, fills up with lake smells and the tinge of burned tinfoil, which means lightning is too near.

Quick steps up the open stairway and my mother's sharp voice: "Get up, Anne. But don't be afraid."

I am not afraid. If my mother says not to be afraid, I am not. This storm is wild and full of strange turns. I feel wide awake and warm.

"Why are we getting up?"

"Storm's bad. Dad wants us downstairs."

I am confused, because if my father wants us downstairs, it means something is wrong. But if my mother has said not to be afraid, then there is nothing to fear. Her voice, *"Now, girl. Get up,"* comes with the next flash. As I hurry from the room, my windows show the silhouetted tree, leaning its sixty years and all its leaves into aluminum light, straining to bend with the wind.

Then my mother is pulling me down the stairs and through the living room, dining room, kitchen—all highlighted in sound, cracking loudly in sudden shimmers.

"Where's the boys?" I ask. The boys sleep upstairs at the end of the hall, farther away from the stairs and closer still to the weather. Their windows look both west and south, down on the new orchard.

"Daddy will get them."

Then down again, pushing open the cellar doors and pulling them shut, quickly down the dark, crooked steps into the basement, past the coal stoker and into the fruit cellar. Here the old stone walls are webbed and cracked, and the sound is abruptly deadened, as though a teacher has clapped for silence. Our breath is fast and dry. My father kicks open the basement doors, barefooted and in his undershorts, carrying two pajama-clad bundles under each large arm. The little girls are already there, wrapped together in blankets, still asleep.

He sets them on the dirt floor, and their toes kick up little puffs of dust. My mother reaches for the boys, pushing them nearer to the little girls. I touch the blue jars on the shelves, running my fingers over glass-shrouded plums and gray meat. One jar clinks against another. The thunder, muffled now, rumbles along the surface of the land. Rick sniffles.

"Shush now," my father says.

It is my first lesson in listening past what is said on the surface of things. To hear weather is to hear the subtext of earth, all that is being said beneath what appears to be said. My father and my mother, both with heads lifted and tipped in that peculiar stance that signals vigilance, listen for some sound past thunder and the crack of lightning, down into the innards of wind. I listen too, regarding for the first time the clamor of air, its gray bellow carrying smells of fields that are not our fields, and the raw odor that close lightning sends out like warning.

"What is it?"

But they are not listening to me.

"Will we lose the tree?" my mother asks.

"If we do, we lose the house too," he says. I can see that. The huge tree grows on the west side and close to our house, a windbreak and afternoon shader. The tree would fall on the house. It would drop, the big trunk crushing first the porch roof, then the roof over my room and the boys' room. The wind picks up. My father moves out of the fruit cellar.

"John, where are you going?" Her voice sounds like an itch.

"Just to take a look. I'll be at the top of the stairs."

My mother pulls the boys close. Tom and I want to follow Dad, but she holds us in that grip that none of us can yet break.

"Is this a tornado?" I try out the word.

"No." She pauses, searches for words. "This is a bad windstorm. But we've had worse. Don't worry."

We can hear better now with the door open: slamming barn doors and rolling cherry buckets and high-pitched wires on the windmill. The steps creak as my father shifts near the door. My father's attention is fierce, like the animals in the barn when they are attacked. His reaction to this weather is new. Until now, weather has been a thick skin folded around me, an extra layer I had grown comfortably into. But this weather had turned our world inside out, making my father seem like a stranger. So why is my mother telling me not to worry?

I feel cold for the first time, tired of the sounds, tired of the blistery anxiety induced by my parents' behavior. When I hear my mother whispering, "Oh please, dear God, keep us safe . . . ," I know for sure the tree will fall on our house. I inhale, ready to wail, when my father's footsteps hurry back down the steps.

"I think it's letting up."

My mother commands, "Rain. Rain."

I swallow the hard place under my throat.

The wind swallows its scream also, and that mute of earth—rain—begins. We listen as it gusts across the fields, slowly resolves to erratic blasts, and finally dies.

At dawn we are tucked into our beds for the second time. *Now I lay me down to sleep.* Curling toward the quiet light that is the other side of night, I think about the prayer: *If I should die before I wake.* I wonder if the wind could have killed us. I know my father was afraid and that my mother may have told a lie, and I wonder if the world talks this way all the time.

In spring I learn new prayers. My parents purchase our first television, a used Zenith. Planes start to fly faster over the farm, bringing new sounds. As the bigger world creeps in on our small, rural one, I try to make sense of it but often fail.

"The sound barrier scared all the cows and they broke out of the pasture," I inform my Aunt Evelyn. "Planes do it on purpose."

"Yes, the red scar is a place where the president hurt himself." I tell my father, who has discussed the red scare with my mother.

"We have a fallout shelter in our basement. It's for Mom to keep her homemade wine," I announce to my teacher.

The fairy tale of the little girl who gets caught in a hell-swamp and the dynamite my father sets to break an old dam both run together in dreams. I learn the word *war* because in school we practice hiding under our desks in case a nuclear attack should occur. I know the neighbor boys have gone into the army because there might be a war. I notice that my father speaks of war with the same voice he uses for storms. But what's a war?

In preparation for first communion, I learn the Act of Contrition, *Oh my God, I am heartily sorry for having offended thee.* My night prayers change, become more difficult and longer. I learn that sin makes God unhappy and that I need to make up for my wrongs. I should never sin, though I have not much hope about this part. I know what stealing is, what meanness is, and what a lie is. It is this last that troubles me most, for it feels like the clay balls I find in the old gravel pit, heavy but slippery, and changeable, depending on who speaks to me and why. Snuffling awarenesses, small mullings happen while I carry jugs of water to the fields or pick beans for supper.

My father grins and scoops us up as he comes in for coffee because once again there has been no frost. Now the time for frost is almost past, and the mornings have been warm and scented. Rain has come when we needed it. The asparagus seedlings in every field are inches tall, and the early radishes in the garden have the bite of a hot summer in them.

My body sizzles with growing, but instead of going to the barns and flopping down in the hay to dream, I creep into the house and sneak past the big washing machine where my mother is running four dozen diapers through the wringer. I slip into the living room, turn on the black-and-white TV, and flip the channel knob. I find no "I Love Lucy," no "Loretta Young," no cartoons. But on one channel a man's voice, speaking the way the priest speaks, catches my ear.

The picture clears. I see an island in a wide gray ocean with some small clouds in the sky. This is how a place would look from an airplane, the way Lake Michigan looks from the bluffs on a big-wind day. The announcer is talking about tests. I know what they are, and I don't like them. I wonder if this island will pass its test.

The music fades, the voice stops. From the TV comes a soft, industrial sound like an old tractor from far away over the hills. At the same time the screen shows a small puff, or maybe it's a round splash, right above the island. *Did someone throw a big stone?*

Then it begins.

The cloud and the sound grow from the ground up, changing slowly to an ongoing thunder until finally it is a sound bigger than a windstorm. All other clouds in the sky look small. From the corner of the couch, I watch as the sky is eaten by this cloud that has one continuous storm in it. I know this is war because it can erase the sky. I see clearly that the sky that gives rain and wind and sun can be obliterated by this other human storm called a bomb.

As the report drones on, I slip my thumb into my mouth. I will not stop sucking until I am past twelve.

That night, after the Act of Contrition for penance, and after the many blessings, my mother comes to tuck me in, and I ask, "Will war come here?"

She does not speak quickly enough, and we both know it. Her brief silence, the pause just before her words, confirms my suspicions.

"No, of course not. War can't come here," she answers, and kisses and tucks. I turn over and face the night sky. I know she has lied. I also understand that she has done this so I won't be afraid. That small pause before her voice returns holds the real truth. And I know from the TV that if war comes, it will be like a tree falling, too big for her or my father to stop. I wake often at night, sweating at the tone of distant planes, fearing that single cloud, larger than any wind. I often pray, "Please God, keep us safe. . . ." But just as I now doubt my mother, I am doubting God. I live closer to my father, closer to his sharp attention to things more powerful than he is.

Metaphor

I am walking home from the one-room schoolhouse down the road, looking down at the damp gravel of the old road, thinking about the thing called reading and trying to figure out how one thing can mean another. I hear the boys shouting and look up to see them careening like kites without wind down the long drive.

"He brought 'em today."

"They're here."

"Hurry up."

The mailman delivers chicks in early spring. The boys, who have been watching for me, come running, hollering down the yard, *Hurry Up!* My mother has commanded that the chicks' boxes may not be opened until I am there too. When I reach the driveway, the boys are jumping, pounding on each other. They are so much alike I cannot hear the differences in their voices. I join them, running with them toward the house, listening to their back-and-forth chatter, scraps of voices on the April wind.

"Chicks. The chicks are here."

"We've got baby chicks."

"They's in the box."

"Two boxes."

"Full of 'em."

Their calls dance back and forth as we move up the driveway and into the house, where, in the back room, the two boxes made of sturdy cardboard reinforced with pieces of white wood rest on the cement floor. The tops of the boxes, plain except for our address, are imprinted with a new word I trace with my finger.

"Leghorns," my mother says for me, coming out of the kitchen, sitting on the rough cement step. And with her sure sense of warning, "You'll scare them to death with all your noise."

We shush each other noisily, barely controlling the taut excitement of our bodies. She lifts one of the boxes so carefully it is as if she is cradling a Christmas ornament. Even so the peeping rises to a startled crescendo. We grab each other, giggling, and follow. I expect her to take them to the barn, but she carries them into the kitchen, then into the dining room and then—an unheard of thing—into the living room, where, just the previous summer, both boys were spanked for bringing in a calf. We know this room is sacred. How can she bring chicks into her living room?

But she does not stop there. We traipse behind her, whispering and bumping into each other's elbows. Where is she going? She carries the chicks past the room serving as Patti's nursery, up the stairs to the second floor, past the room where Marijo, the toddler, is napping, down the long hall with the bend in the middle, until she finally toes open the door of the southwest room. It is a shabby room, and because of the long hall without a light, we cannot yet go there without shuddering. The room is in need of repair, the old wallpaper half torn off and the plaster falling. But when we enter I am stunned. She has taken pieces of masonite and propped them up and taped them together with cardboard gussets at the places that don't fit perfectly so that now the sunny half of the room contains a large cage, six by eight feet square and two feet high. On the floor my mother has spread tar paper as well as layers and layers of old newspaper. In the middle there is a cheap lamp with a metal hood suspended from binder twine. It is lit and shines directly onto the newspaper in a bright circle of warmth. Near it is a low feed box and a metal water tank with a circular trough.

The chicks will live upstairs!

She smiles at our astonishment as she carefully lowers the box into the cage.

"It's warmer here," she says by way of explanation. She steps into the cage and squats.

"Watch," she says. "Everyone will get a turn."

She takes her pocket knife and slits the sealing tape along the sides. We watch, nearly trembling, as she inserts her fingers into the air holes and lifts the lid. When she does, the box wiggles and the cheeping rises once again, and our bodies are like small toys, wound up and trembling to their tiny music.

She lifts the cover and moves it to the side, and there they are. The interior of the box is divided into four sections, each one containing a dozen chicks. They are fluffy, with tiny beaks and eyes, and talons that spread out beneath them like prehistoric fingers. They are so small that we love them immediately, and our voices are a momentary babble, begging her *please, please.* Her large hands hover over the sections, then drop into one. She brings together both hands under a single chick and lifts it like a delicate offering, as if she were cupping water that she must not spill. Her care and the fragility of the chick fill us with privilege and fear.

"Make your hands like mine."

We do, folding the fingers of one hand inside the fingers of the other. Tom gets it mixed up, trying to lace his fingers together as though for cat's cradle, and we have to untangle them and get it right before we are all ready, our faces for once united. We are like candles, half radiant, half solemn, and she slowly places the first one into Rick's still baby-like hands.

"Make it feel warm," she whispers.

Rick bends his head and breathes on it, and it sinks into a soft puff of down nestled in his tiny palms. Then she drops her hand into the box again and brings up one for Tom and finally one for me. We stand, three children in new awe, shoulder to shoulder with each other, seamless in our breathing, staring at this fragment of bone and fluff in our palms. I cannot tell where the chick in my hands ends and the skin of my own body begins.

One poops on Tom's hand. He drops it, and it flaps its stunted wings and cheeps pitifully. My mother scolds, and everything is a flurry until the chick is rescued. She takes it up and holds it, looking it over. Finally, as it seems not to have suffered any harm, she moves her hands under the heat lamp, opens her palms like two wings, and lets the chick slide gently between them onto the artificial heat, where it sways, takes a step or two, and sways again. Then, as the heat penetrates its layer of down, it stops. Its eyelids come up like a cloud over its black specks of eyes, and it dozes in the heat.

For the next hour we take turns, carefully lifting the chicks and placing them under the heat lamp. There is a trick to catching them without hurting them. One chick slips from a hand and is held too long by the leg, struggling between thumb and forefinger; when it is finally put down it tries to walk but falls over again and again. She puts it quickly aside where we cannot see it. And once, when the second box is opened, one of the chicks is on its side, eyes closed. I ask, "Is it sleep-ing?"

"No, it's dead."

"Why does it look like it's sleeping?"

She places that one aside too, sighing, "It just does."

I watch the injured one and the dead one in the corner. Something tugs at me, something about the meaning of this death, this injury, but I do what I have already learned to do. I turn to the living.

The chicks thrive in the old bedroom. The early spring sun keeps the room warmer in the daytime, and when the nights are cold they gather like a pale yellow cloud under the heat of the metal hood. After school I run up the stairs, lean over the partition, pick one up, and nuzzle it. The chicks become a transition from school, where my loneliness makes me nervous and inattentive, to the time when I am once again enveloped by the farm, where things have only one meaning.

I listen to their cheeping, the sounds they make when they feed on the warm mush my mother slops into the troughs, their tiny beaks clicking against the lip of metal. I begin to hear these as individual sounds, like letters. Later, the claws, beginning their instinctive scratching at the newspaper, seem to make a word: chittle, chittle, chittle—a word that seems secret, but I pretend to understand.

Since the room where the chicks live shares a wall with the one where I sleep, I sometimes hear them cheeping their words through the old iron register that opens to both rooms. One at a time, as they drift off, they cheep here and there, like the very end of rain. Once I am awake late into the night when one of them cheeps frantically, as though it were having a bad dream, and the others all wake and cheep together madly for a few moments. It is as though they have to speak the dream, then discuss it all over again before they can rest. I wonder if their dream means something. After a while I whisper to them, *It's all right, you're all right,* using the words my parents have used to comfort me.

Their perfection does not last. Soon they begin to develop wings and lose their down. They take on a gangly look as their pinfeathers elongate and change from pale yellow to fleshy white, making them look awkward. Some evolve the red slash down the forehead, the longer, more vivid combs marking the roosters. Over the weeks they live in the house, they become mean and begin pecking at the others. My mother announces that it is time to move them all to the coop.

We shove them into bushel crates and boxes and drag them in our toy wagon up to the north end of the barnyards. I believe they will be lonely in the coop, that they will die so far away from the house. My mother ignores me as she scrubs the room clean. Then, adding insult to injury, she announces that the walls will be repaired and papered, the floors painted, and the windows caulked. My brothers will move into this room in the fall. They're old enough now.

One morning my mother tells me I should begin looking for pullet eggs.

"Plute eggs?"

"Pullet. They should start laying eggs any day now," she says, as she pours hot wax onto strawberry jam.

"What are pullet eggs?"

"Little ones. Before they can make big ones, they make a few little ones for practice. Go on. Go see."

"I don't feel like it."

My mother sighs at this new stubbornness—not the first time she has struggled with it—but says, "Maybe you'll be lucky."

Why is it, even as a child, I want to believe in luck?

The coop is a long low building. The east end consists of a workshop, full of tools and tires and the new welder Dad has been working on. The west room has rows and rows of tiny windows, and inside there is a low shelf with half a dozen roosting poles braced above it. Along the south side, crates have been tied to each other and nailed roughly against the wall, then set with straw. Here and there a few of the young hens have begun to nest. But today they are all out in the yard, scratching and making a sound like the low creak of a squeaky door. I search the nests like a young animal, nosing into the straw, eager for luck, but there are no pullet eggs anywhere. Then, as I turn away, I see that in the opposite corner Dad has stacked extra bales of straw. With the sure intuition of a child, I know that there will be crevices and straw shallows where a young hen could nest. I climb a few of the bales, and there, nestled in a hollow, I find one small egg.

It is white!

I have only known brown eggs, the dark, earth-toned ones of the older, heavier breeds. But this is white. On a farm, where there is always dust, manure, chaff, grime, and soils so varied they are like a color wheel of dirt, I understand that it is a miracle to discover something this white. Even milk seems gray by comparison.

So this is what luck looks like.

I stare at the small white sphere for a while. It is connected to all that is good in the world. There, on all fours in the straw, looking down at a small white egg, I understand I have been blessed, that I am different from the rest of my brothers and sisters because I have found this white egg. It means something more than what it is. This white egg is lucky, and it means I am lucky. I feel as though this has always been true. It will always be true.

I curl my hand under it but, as often happens in the first laying, it is so fresh that it is still sticky with blood on its underside. As I turn it in my hand, some of the blood spots my fingers and my palm.

The egg is bleeding!

I drop it. It cracks open, and there is the tiny yolk, now broken and spreading across the straw. I stare at the cracked white shells, at the broken yolk in its clear syrup, and at the blood on my hand.

If finding the egg means something about luck and good fortune, then breaking it also means something, but what that meaning is frightens me, slips through my fingers.

My mother asks, "Did you find any?"

"No. There weren't any."

It is my first lie, one told out of fear, not of her punishment, but out of not wanting to look at what happens at the moment when one event leads to another, becomes something else, when good fortune is broken, is not sleeping but dead. It is a lie I tell because I cannot acknowledge out loud what my body has grown into—that meaning extends, that one thing comes to mean another, that if a perfect white shell means good fortune, then it means something else to have blood on my fingers, a broken golden yolk in the straw. I have read something, and understanding is beginning to jump out of the land, out of all the small practices like gathering eggs.

Cleaning Kill

In the fall, over-ripe pears drop from the trees, and the scent of fermented fruit rises from the grass. Sniffing deeply and dizzy with winey air, I stumble over the rotting pears. Sometimes I pick one up and stare at the oddly mottled, green and gold skin. I pierce the soft pulp with a stick. I make little people of the pears, plunging twig arms and legs into the bulbous pear bodies. Where I add the appendages, the broken skin releases the scent of fruit. I salivate and eat the pears.

I can't climb the pear trees because the lowest branches grow too high on the trunks. The trees are old, planted by the farm's original owners, and they have been left to grow wild in our front yard. I love these trees both because I love pears and because we don't harvest them seriously. They rank with the sugar maples and pines, trees without immediate purpose, trees that don't make life harder. I stare up through gnarled, unpruned branches and try to catch windfalls. After the fall, I stand among the rotting pears so long that their odor overwhelms my nose, then disappears, becoming no scent at all.

They never cut down the pear trees because during deer hunting season the hunters hung their kill from them. The branches were so high and thick the dogs couldn't reach the carcasses. All through November, the men let the meat age there. Because this spot was in the front yard, hanging the kill was also an invitation. I remember other hunters stopping, pulling their trucks into the driveway, their red-and-black plaid hunting overalls smudged with field dirt.

"Nice buck, John. Where'd you get it?"

"Out by Potawatomi."

"In the swamp?"

"Yep, south side, just on the edge of thicket there."

"You must not had to track him. You get in that swamp, you can't track, it's so thick."

"Yep."

"Brought him right down."

"Well. I think he'd been driven a bit. Seemed tired, so it was easier."

"How many points?"

"Oh, ten or so."

"Nice rack. Wha'd he dress at?"

"Oh, I don't know. Around one-twenty."

People liked to talk with my dad because he didn't brag. He'd tell them the rack was ten points when they could see it was twelve, or he'd say the buck dressed at one-twenty when it looked and probably was bigger. He carried a small hunting knife tucked in his pocket, not the big, triumphant blades many men wore on their belts. Sometimes I would slip this slim, neat jackknife out of his hunting jacket and turn it over and over in my hands, touching the dark hilt. It smelled like his large hands. Because he never made a big deal about being a good hunter, the other hunters weren't intimidated while they looked at the kill and crushed the rotting pears under their boots. I loved to watch my father and listen to his talk. I never saw the kill, not really. But the scent of it was there.

On a late Thanksgiving afternoon, I wander out to the pear trees. I am scuffing through the remnants of fruit, looking for a pear that is not too soft or wormy, one that I can eat out here in the quiet. The farmhouse is buzzing with my mother, aunts, cousins, and the hustling preparation for dinner. All day the luxurious pumpkin and the tangy sage have been in my nose. My stomach growls, but my nose hunts for something sweeter.

The younger cousins have gone to the barns while the women hold dinner because the men are still hunting. The men are in a stage of desperateness because one uncle, who has come all the way from Illinois, has not killed his deer, and he doesn't want to go back empty-handed. If they aren't lucky, they will come home at first dark. If they are lucky, it will be later (because they must drag out the carcass), but my mother's voice will be like fire.

I sit down at the base of a pear tree, looking around at the mounds of pears, yellow and black this late in the season. I can feel the scent surrounding me in the still dusky air. I pick one, frost bitten and thawed. I bite it, and it tastes tingly. I chew, spit, and watch the road where the big pickups will come careening over the gravel.

It is not a long wait, not quite dark. The trucks, honking success, roar up the slope of the front yard. They pull directly under the bigger tree, tires sliding and spraying crushed pears and wet grass. One truck backs under a high, heavy branch, and another parks facing it so the headlights shine on the tree and the work. They plug utility lights into the cigarette lighters of the cabs and hang these lights on the trunk of the tree. Rangy shadows cleave the yard.

My brothers leap down from the cabs and run to the house, announcing the kill. "Got 'em, right through the neck. Big buck." They are screaming for approval from the women. I hear shushing and the remark, "Aren't we lucky?" The distant thudding of kitchen doors is renewed as the women reorganize the meal's timing. My mother flicks the lights in the dining room to signal she knows.

I lean quietly against the fender. No one notices me. The men move with powerful, heavy steps, full of booted purpose and an authority laced with urgency. So many pears have been crushed under the wheels that the scent, resting quietly in the cold, rises sharply.

My father climbs out of his truck, a loop of rope over his arm. He pulls the tailgate down and leaps into the truck bed. In the headlights of the other truck, he casts an enormous shadow toward the house. He bends, lifts. I see the flash of horns visible over the bed, then he is looping an end of rope, tying and tying. He throws the loose end of the rope over the high branch, and the other two men catch it, their arms also casting huge, sharp shadows. They pull. The rope squeals as they hoist the buck, horns first, toward the thick, black hand of the branch. The carcass rises slowly in the artificial light, joining the tree, hanging like a slim, frost-killed blossom. Its legs dangle loosely. The deer has a wide, graceful set of antlers and a big gray ruff; even in this light its hide is a warmer brown than usual.

"Been corn-fed to get that color?" Uncle Eddy asks in his nervous way.

"Oh prob'ly, that or winter wheat, some kind of grain." My father's voice is steady.

The body twists in the light. I see for the first time the cut in the lower stomach, the length of my arm, running parallel to the backbone.

My brothers come sliding back from the house. They see me in the dark and move closer, strange and wild.

"What's that?" I ask softly, pointing to the opening.

"They took out the stomach and the 'testines already."

"What are they gonna do now?"

"Gut it. They got to finish gutting it so it don't get poisoned."

My father barks some command at the boys and they dash to him, slipping in the pears. Rick reaches out and touches the dark, perfectly shaped hoof. My father's voice takes on a careful tone.

"Now watch. You ain't gonna do this for a while yet, but you need to get how it's done."

The men in the bed of the truck lean against the buck's backbone, stabilizing the carcass, and my father takes the small hunting knife from his pocket, unfolds and locks it. He places the knife at the bottom of the cut and slices down deeply between the animal's legs. He opens the slit and the men come round, holding flashlights. Something dark begins to drip between their legs and feet. His hands move into the cavity. He cuts slowly, then reaches in and pulls out bulbous, dark, strangely shaped things which he names. His face tightens.

"You got to take out this, the colon and the rectum. It's got manure in it, and it'll make the meat rot if it's not taken clean. You got to try not to hit a deer in the stomach because it doesn't kill 'em clean, and it makes a mess of their insides. You don't want none of these organs to break. This here's the bladder—don't ever want to break that, gets piss all down the meat—and the gallbladder, that's bad too." His huge hands move in and out, the knife moving surely, darkly, no longer glinting. When they break the pelvis, I hear the bone crack, and they take clean lath slats and force them inside the body to prop the cavity open wider.

"You got to put these sticks in so the meat cools faster. Faster it cools, the less spoilage, better it ages."

"Now here's the liver. It's good we got it whole." He sets it on a clean handkerchief on the side of the truck. My mother will slice and pickle all the sweetbreads.

He places the knife at the bottom of the cut, tips it precisely, rips all the way to the neck. Gently, he feels for bone, finds the rib cage and splits the ribs, spreading them. He begins to cut through thin gray tissue that looks like sheer fabric. "This here's membrane and the diaphragm, you cut it out to get the lungs." He removes the oddly shaped globules, gray and dark. Then he is holding something fist-solid in his hands. He sets the heart aside with the liver.

As he and the men work, they drop the mess over the side into a big, metal cherry bucket. I sneak toward it, wanting to see, afraid but fascinated. I am drunk on fermented pears and an unexpected kinship with shadows, blood, and efficiency. I slip in the dark, bang against the truck and fall, smelling rotten fruit and frozen grass. I am even smaller here, nearly invisible in the rot and dark, but hungry for what they are doing. I move slowly.

They begin the washing. My brothers have half dragged, half carried cherry buckets full of water from the outside spigot. My father lifts the buckets, spilling cold water on his pants and boots. He sloshes water into the cavity of the buck, rinsing the inside of the carcass, rinsing and rinsing and rinsing out dirt and chunks of flesh and fat.

Talk has stopped, but the work is full of sound: the slap of water, the odd gush as it sluices back from inside the rib cage, splattering their bodies and the bed of the truck, then dripping down the tailgate. As he flings the last full bucket of water into the cavity, I reach the pail. I bend over to peer at what they have tossed aside, and as I do I am splashed with the bloody water.

What is inside the pail is crawly and ugly, with shapes that no longer have meaning. Whatever care the men took in removing these things from the body has been negated in the tossing aside. And it reeks. As I lean over the pail, the smell of bile and manure, the underlying scent of sour grain, and—more than any other—the scent of blood rises like a hand against my face. I am nauseated by the stink and pull away, gagging. The scent is so strong and thick I feel sticky with it. I sit back in the grass. I grab a pear and breathe it in deeply, wanting to chase away the death scent. But the pear is changed too, its scent mixed now with the stench of the offal pail, no longer pure, thus no longer soothing.

Huddled in the cold, I feel the deer hanging from the pear tree, the smell of manure and blood, the pears softening and freezing. The soft yellow fruit will always be mixed with killing. And the scent of offal is a broken blessing into my father's way: the hunting, the butchering, the providing. I feel a hollowness rinsed with clarity. I am washed out with the knowledge that what hangs in the dark also feeds me.

Interruptions

Sunday dinners around the old Duncan Phyfe table are so ritualized they are like ceremonies, riddled with chatter and the lively, strained language of families. The ritual of Sunday dinner consists of jokes so old they belong in encyclopedias. It is filled with predictable tensions. A person learns to tiptoe over the decades, the quirks and vital criticisms that no one forgets—no matter how petty—and no one talks about.

Alternate weeks my mother serves baked ham with scalloped potatoes or fried chicken with parsley-mashed potatoes to a table full of relatives and five kids. She is a brilliant if sometimes impatient hostess. She will pull chickens from the freezer before church and serve them with a high flourish before three, but she may not be happy about it.

We are expected to help. To make the table long enough for Grandpa Joe, Aunt Mary, Grandma Julia, Uncle Joe, or any of a dozen others, we pull apart the two halves of the table and fit the dark "leaves" into the gap in the middle. Over that we spread heavy, white-lined, reinforced "protectors," though why these are placed over the wood on Sundays and no other day confuses me. These protectors remind me of giant maps. I am intrigued with how they fan open like Jacob's ladder.

One day when I am alone in the house, I squeeze into the narrow closet next to the refrigerator and reach into the skinny darkness of brooms and mops and pull out these heavy panels the width of the table.

I unfold them onto the floor and get the box of broken crayons. On my stomach I examine this wide expanse of cream emptiness. I pick up the green crayon. I draw trees: the great silver maple in the front yard, the orchard trees, and the crab apples in the backyard. I pick up other colors. I draw the barns and the chicken coop and the lilac bushes. I change colors, adding browns, oranges, yellows, blues. I draw in proportion with the size of my canvas. I do not draw the house because I don't understand the house yet.

The kitchen door opens and closes, grocery bags scuffle on the formica, and a few steps clack across the floor. My mother's sharp gasp knifes across the room: "What are you doing?" I feel her strong hand on my shoulder, her scolding, telling me crayons don't wash off, that I should know better, that I'm the oldest and should set an example.

I loved drawing on the protectors because there was an abundance in their size that rarely occurred in our household, except on Sundays. Every time after that when I set the table, I lift the linen to peek at the trees, which do not come off despite my mother's hardest scrubbing. Sometimes at dinner, as the talk passes back and forth over my head, I look at the tablecloth. If Rick or Tom has spilt water, the crayon marks show through the damp spot like pale lines on a map.

Over the protectors, mother places white linens which, though sometimes stained and frayed, make the table elegant and so uncharacteristic of our lives that we are often better behaved simply because of how it looks. On the linen she spreads yellowed, carefully starched lace. This makes a shadow pattern better than branches on fresh snow. Finally, over that, we are allowed to place settings of chipped china, in a soft floral pattern, that is used only on Sundays. It is, she tells us with a lift in her voice, her wedding china.

In the kitchen she is stirring gravy or basting the ham, which is dotted with a spice we call gloves, not cloves, because each little seed looks like the finger of a tiny glove. Activity accelerates as the meal comes closer: potatoes to be mashed by strong arms, bread to be cut, a bowl of greens to be tossed, serving spoons, extra coffee, sugar and milk.

The meal begins with blessing ourselves over folded hands, and a murmur like old rain, "Bless us, old Lord, and these thy gifts." It continues with my father's hands lifting the platter of chicken or carving the apple-pink ham from the bone, yellow fat glistening inside the rind. If it's a ham Sunday, the meat is placed on an oval platter with pink flowers; if it's a chicken Sunday, the roast is placed on a large round one, decorated with sheaves of wheat.

Among the hands that pass over my head, there are no beauties, not one unmarked by overwork. Whether these are the hands of men or women, their knuckles rise like knots; thumbs come the size of hammer handles, and fingers mimic the wide tines of tools. The skin is rough as the fields' surface in spring, torn with small wounds or thin and shiny with age and sun. Fingernails are always chipped and rarely clean. Palms are a curved bowl of calluses. They are hungry hands, hands without much gentleness, but they pass the food over my head with the certainty and confidence they have about nothing else in their lives. They serve creamed beans and stewed tomatoes onto the plates of children as though they had practiced no other thing in their lives. They spread butter. They dish and scoop, and, with a deftness past precision, they cut meat and feed, chewing and swallowing and smacking.

After the first rush, the small gossip begins, punctuated by the gentle phrases of people who, on other days, curse comfortably.

"Darlene will marry the Gray boy."

"You don't say."

"The Smith family is moving to Muskegon."

"I declare."

They take in small news and small pickles with the same appetite. I watch them, and I eat too, feeling their attentions move and shift and focus—intense interest in the scarlet hue of beets mixed with opinions about which pup from that last litter of beagles seems most promising.

It is the rustling chorus of human beasts at their greatest event—not a mass, not an inauguration, but Sunday dinner.

After these meals, the other kids slip away like quick fish. They will return later for pie, but after a half hour of being in one place, they wiggle in bursts and spasms. Their games call: hide and seek or front yard baseball. But I am allowed, if I can remain quiet and not spill anything, to stay and listen. As much as the eating, it is the talk I desire. I am curious about these people. From their Sunday afternoon conversations, I learn there is a family that existed before, a history that came before the one I can see and taste in the fields, and they open the door into it. Their talk is like that of poets practicing rare associations—the story of the tractor getting stuck last spring leads to the story of Joe's horse mired in the bog at Potawatomi Swamp, which leads to comparing the best places for picking huckleberries. Each small narrative is bridged to the next by mere slips of conjunctions.

I hunger for these stories as these people have hungered for this meal. I love best when my father says, "I'm not sure, but I think it happened like this." I know this gives him permission to tell the story more adventurously. He is in the middle of telling a story I love, about the first little girl who lived on the farm—a girl who was the oldest in another family, the one before ours—who tore all the leaves off the sapling that grew to be our own silver maple.

"She stripped off its leaves," he says. "Left it bare as a suckling pig."

This for my benefit. I giggle every time. Then he gets to the good part.

"They thought the tree would die," he says.

I see the tree shriveling, the leaves turned to small green snippets. I wonder what made her do what she did, but I want the tree to live. I wait to hear the words that will tell me the tree lived. I need this ending, this righting of wrong. Endless possibility.

My mother interrupts. "Now John, when was that? Do you know the year?" The story stops. All the faces at the table turn to her, the woman whose family has been here even longer than my father's, who can see back to the century before this one. The silence pulls back their faces, turns their features inward as they look through the years for a reference point—someone's birthday, some change, the war, the flu epidemic, the war again—running their fingers over the looseness of history to something that will make the story stay in place. I see them struggle. This thing of the past is big and slippery, so there is never any argument about whether her question is important or not. These things must be clear. But the coffee cools, the pie remains untouched. They look at each other, the story unfinished.

My mother interrupts again, calculating. "Well, she's in her eighties now, and she couldn't have been more than ten."

They nod.

"So, do you think it was '90 or '95?"

"Well, the big barn wasn't finished until 1900."

"Was the big barn built yet or not?"

"I don't believe it was."

"Then it could have been in '90."

"Mother, do you think that's about right?" Mom turns to one of the grandmas.

"No, I think it was earlier. She was born in '82, so she would have been eight or older then." Grandma Julia speaks enthusiastically about these dates.

"Too old for that kind of silliness." Grandpa chimes.

"If she was born in '82, how old was she when she pulled the leaves off?" My mother turns to my dad.

He pauses, "I think she was five, maybe six when she had the tantrum."

Tantrum. It was a tantrum? He never said this before.

"So the tree was stripped in '87 or '88." My mother concludes so firmly that everyone at the table nods with satisfaction.

Underneath the lace tablecloth, in my lap, my hands sweat. Why does she do this? Why does she have to stop the story? She interrupts every time. My mother pays attention to times and years and the exact name of every person in the neighborhood. When things happen, how they happen, who married whom, when they gave birth, when the children were baptized, when they married, when they died and of what.

"Her name was Ida," my mother says suddenly. "Her maiden name was Cotton. And her mother's name was Hattie." She says this tenderly, as she might say her own maiden name, Van Agtmeal.

"And I believe her mother married a Peterson. She was born in 1858," Grandma finishes.

They, especially my mother, hold the history of our world: not its mysteries but its exactness.

I want my father's voice back. I want him to finish the less certain story, where the girl has no name yet, and we don't know exactly how old she is when she is so angry she pulls all the leaves off the tree. I want him to say how the leaves came back, tiny golden leaves, how it blossomed and thrived, and how now, nearly a hundred years later, it remains strong and green. I want the possibilities.

But this is my mother's pattern. One of the clan tells a story, she interrupts, and everything halts, suspended as they all explore time and tack it into place.

It is the Fourth of July, and the grass has not cooled, even though our shadows stretch from the well-pit down the sloping yard almost to the end of the patchy oval. Dust hangs over the driveway, a nomadic haze from every elephantine Chevy that rolls down the gravel road. As each car disappears, the dust roils and drifts under the maple or among the pear trees or over the barnyard, a sleepy cloud. The hum of the bees, who now have a nest in the wall of the house where the eaves meet the porch, sounds thick and clotted with heat.

I am sitting at the well-pit with my feet in a cherry bucket of water when Tom slouches out of the house, slamming the screen door. He looks at me: "We can't go."

"I told you."

"We got no money."

"She said that yesterday."

"Why they have to charge for fireworks anyway?"

"I guess it costs to put them on."

Suddenly he turns. "You shut up." And he kicks over the bucket.

Rick comes out, carrying a handful of radishes. He pops them into his mouth one at a time and crunches loudly, as if they were broken hopes.

"She's got sparklers."

"She don't." Tom is sure.

"She said if she got some help with dishes, we could light them when Dad gets home."

"He's gotta work overtime."

"She says he'll be home at dark."

"That's hours away."

"Sparklers, that'd be good." Rick is imagining.

"Yeah, but it's a long time to wait," Tom mutters.

They look like twin dolls with different mechanical abilities, one nodding slowly, one shaking his head.

After the dishes are done, we play hide-and-seek in the orchard grasses. The game is a dance, in and out of the regularity of trees plant-ed in rows. We race for the porch to be safe. We are so close in age and growth that we are always able to tag each other. No one ever gets home safe. We know each other's hiding places because we know each other and the land that shapes us—the crotch of the crab apple tree, the stone pile on the edge of the orchard, the burdock patch down by the one-room schoolhouse.

Finally Mother drifts out onto the stone front porch and sits on the bottom step in the shade of the spirea bushes. She has the slim red-and-white boxes with her. She sets them next to her on the step. Every time one of us races for home, we beg her, "Let us light them now."

"No. Wait for your Dad."

I see her waiting too, listening for the drone of the old car coming from the south, from Blackmer's store where he meets the carpool that brings him from Montague, that mysterious city an hour away where he works all day before he comes home and eats and then goes to the fields or barns until dark. I see her face, the watchfulness in it. She is not paying much attention to us; she is waiting for him, for his presence. There is tension and ripeness in her.

Finally the car turns up the driveway and stirs a new cloud of dust into the yard. Tonight, rather than parking in the clear place next to the grape arbor, he pulls into the yard. When he steps out she hangs back, looking at him while we rush him, wild bodies grabbing legs and arms, pulling on his big hands, laughing and screaming if he tickles or crushes us against his thighs, or picks us up and holds us upside down as we laugh and gasp and struggle against this man whose touch we can never get enough of. He puts us down, releasing us with a soft chant. "All right, all right now, easy, take it easy." But even as he says these words he is looking at her and walking toward her, and my brothers are leaping onto the porch and around the spirea and squealing in high voices: "Sparklers, now the sparklers. We want the sparklers."

She reaches for them but stops. She looks at him, smiling, and asks, "How's your day?"

I can't believe it.

Then she asks, "Did you get the flour from the store?"

I am appalled. How can she do this, how can she interrupt the forward motion to the sparklers, to the wild light which by now has taken on such dimension we will all burst if we cannot have sparklers?

Finally she gives him the boxes, and he opens them and places them on the broken stone at the bottom of the steps. He takes out the battered silver Zippo and turns away from us to use his body to block this first light.

And she tells us, "Look at the dark part of the sky."

In the west it is not dark. The shards of summer sunset still hover there. But in the east it is nearly full dark, with that springing blue coming up iridescent quick, pulling night from the horizon. "Look at the dark part of the sky," she says again.

Because we are not looking at the fading west but to the eastern night—quiet and staring, searching for some star not yet visible—when he turns with the sparkler in his hands and holds it up like a scepter, it catches our vision. As though we are connected by strings, we turn to him. And because we have been looking at the darkest part of the sky, the sparkler seems more luminous than it should have been at this time of evening. It trails white gold as he wafts it over our heads, over our hard look into the darkness.

We are wild with eagerness, wild for more, but each time he bends to the tip of the gray wand, she stops him, "Oh, John, wait." Then she looks at us and says, "Look away." Or she pulls Marijo close to her, wrapping her legs playfully around her, and says, "Close your eyes." We all close our eyes, and he places the slim glittering wands into our hands. Then she says, "Open your eyes."

We scream and run, shaggy-haired firemoths fluttering over the yard, our faces foreign with the thrill and our glittering, sweating energy. We draw pictures in the darkness, swinging the wands high over our heads in dizzying circles. We clutter the dark with our bright names scrawled in letters. The broken signatures hang alive in the air for a few brief seconds before they fade.

Once, returning for another sparkler, I catch him looking at her. The flash of my dying sparkler highlights for just a moment what is astonishing about them. I see bravery I have no words for, and then I hear her voice asking him to wait again, and I see also the utter gentility of him doing that, his face toward hers, smiling a little, his hand poised, holding the moment, holding the anticipation of light for just this moment before she permits him to strike another slim, short-lived sparkler.

The darkness overtakes them, spitting, as the sparkler dies. Light dies on their faces with the image of them, poised in the moment of an interruption, burning into my retinas. They stay there, hovering for so long that I have time to get this scene into my head, what it feels like to wait in a moment, to feel the break between things. It is the moment held and radiant, a power she had which I had missed.

I tell you, I long for her questions, the breathless space before the story begins again, before the sparkler burns down to the inevitable end. Oh, Mama, interrupt again. Make time stop. Make the teller, the one with the light in his hands, wait for the briefest space. While the ham cools or the pies dry out, while we hungrily hang over the porcelain or run over the grass, delay the momentum of dark gathering. Let us look at it before the answers come, before the light returns and binds us once again to the dazzling, forward-moving stories.

Liturgy

My father's call, *Come boss, come boss,* was the first litany of my childhood. He was the one who called the cows, and my first memories of him are in the lane herding them to be milked: a herd of big, restless cows, their black-and-white hides caked with manure, their great dark eyes stupid with grass and the chewing of summer.

Once, as the cattle swayed and rattled in the basement of the barn, I remember hearing his steps moving among the mows on the upper floor, forking the hay down like a grass waterfall through dark chutes. I remember the stone foundation littered with cracks, the rusty stanchions, the feeding troughs. I remember the big stainless steel milkers and the way his hands washed the teats before slipping on the cups, the sigh and snort of cattle with their mouths in water bowls, belch of cud, soft rustle of nuzzled straw, the sharp, heavy smell of manure.

His voice talking to cows was a benediction, with elements of a circus sideshow. For a cow who was slow to move, he would slap the flat of his hand to the accompaniment of monosyllables, insisting she take her place in the stanchions. "Hey, eeeiie, git, git over boss, over boss." Soothing a nervous heifer, he would sing "Hey girl, hey girl." For a long time, because he used the same words when he comforted me, I thought he knew only one way of speaking.

When I talk with people about the language of my childhood, I often think of prayer. The first prayers I learned were the Catholic blessing and grace: "Bless us, oh Lord, and these thy gifts." In my memory, this is a prayer accompanied by chaos.

Patti bangs her spoon on the chrome tray of the high chair. Tom kicks the pedestal of the table over and over. Marijo hums, looking anxiously from one to another of her siblings. Rick pats the dog; the dog grunts. My mother and father have been arguing, not always good-naturedly. More than half the time there are hired hands or neighbor kids at the table—and strange animals under it.

Once everyone is seated my mother begins by blessing herself, her long hand waving in the air like a wing: forehead, *Father*, chest, *Son*, one shoulder, *Holy*, the second shoulder, *Ghost*. Folding her hands, she passes the words to Dad, as though she is only the preliminary act. And he begins, *Bless us, oh Lord*. We all chime in, Tom racing forward, trying to beat Rick to the amen, me making faces at them as I try to say it perfectly—*and these Thy gifts*—Marijo lagging behind, saying the words by rote and with only half her attention, Patti muttering soft baby sounds, trying to be part of this gesture too: *which we are about to receive . . .* rolling on like a row of hills in our mouths.

I always thought the most important words were the first ones, the ones in my father's voice, *Bless us, oh Lord*. The *oh Lord*, the way my father said it—in what I now know was humility, perhaps with a bone tiredness so deep it was like plow's teeth—that phrase from my father's mouth, and then my mother's voice joined with his *from Thy bounty*, is a sound like two notes finding each other in the midst of dissonance. The words stopped meaning anything and evolved into a half song caught in my mind, something like the way we plant tiny spring seeds, over and over, down and in and fold over the dirt and pat softly, pat, and down and over, on and on.

After the dairy herd failed, my father bought beef cattle, some-times the red-brown ones, sometimes the black Angus with their white faces and beautiful black eyes. Though he no longer called them down the lane to be milked, he walked among them—slapping, running his hands along their backbones as he stepped into the herds, checking, always checking. Listening, listening to them breathe, that sound when they are all in a barn, the big lungs working easily in the dark of their thick bodies.

On one of those nights in late fall, while listening to the cows, he first hears the wheeze. He has been hunting in the cold all day. He isn't sure at first that the soft whistle is not his own tired breath running oddly into his ears, is that of another animal, or something else under the air full of hay and belched cud. He can barely hear it, the sound a hot old pot makes as the heating element burns off the crud. He leaves the barn light on for them, turns uneasily as grass in wind, and walks back up to the house. The next night, he is sure, and the day after, he picks up the phone and dials the vet.

All through late November and December he and my brothers bat-tle the infection. They build a wooden cage with a chute. It stands at the mouth of the barn where the cattle are housed. Every morning they run the cattle out of the barn into the barnyard. The animals are too sick to resist. One by one they drive them up the chute into the cage, then tie them into place. They pull the gate up to lock them in, and with syringes the length of rulers, my father and brothers pierce the skin and plunge bright orange fluid into the cattle's rumps.

A few of the animals start to feel better. They fight the chute, the cage, the plunging needles. The boys and Dad take turns, one pulling the cow in with ropes, smacking it with twine, prodding it with wooden boards. The animals kick, lowing into the air, then coughing a terrible, agonizing retch, as though the inside of the world would come up.

"Hiya! Hiya! Get back you sonabitch." The pine board slams against the cow's shin as my brothers force the animal up the chute. The animal barely moves.

"Again. Hit 'em again." Groaning, my father pulls the rope as he stands at the head of the chute. He drags the cow. My brother pushes and slaps the cow with the board. After two more aching swings, the animal's hooves scrape against the wood slats of the chute. The cow stumbles in, bawling that high whine: a small engine going bad; the cooling apparatus is dead, and it's winding up, running faster and faster. My brother climbs the chute, syringe in hand, and plunges it down with all his strength into the dark hide. The animal rears angrily, butting wildly against the chute, the gate, my father's knees.

When he reads the Bible story on Christmas Eve, the Advent candles and the tree lights are the only illumination in the room. He holds the black family Bible, open to the New Testament, so that it curves in his hands like two hills. He tips the book toward the candlelight, lifting his head a little but never his voice. He reads as slowly as spring comes. I never listen to the church prayers that follow but, kneeling on the living room floor, I am lost in the imagery he conjures with his voice.

The attempt to save the cattle has been going on every day for a month. Two animals have died, and on this morning I wake at dawn in the room with the window that looks down on the barns and their yards. I hear my mother's and father's voices wafting up with the bitter scent of cheap coffee. They are arguing, but softly.

"Do you have to do it today? Can't you wait?"

"They're suffering."

"I know, but does it matter if they're going to die anyway?"

"I'll do it now. The kids won't hear."

"It'll wake them. I know it will."

"The boys know already. What difference will it make?"

"It's Christmas."

The door closes. My mother's cup comes down on the table with a resigned click.

I get up then and go down, and my mother tells me what is going to happen, that I should go back to bed and try to sleep. I am standing in the archway between the dining and living rooms, and I see her silhouetted by the dim light through the dining-room windows, her head sunk against the back of her fist, her graying hair illuminated a bit, the shadows on her face a sad combination of cool planes. Beyond that, through the windows, the roofs of the barns are covered with new snow.

In the bedroom, I pull the pillow to the end of the bed, wrap the sunburst quilt around me, and crack the old window open until the cold air hits my face.

Making small, dark tracks in the snow, my father crosses from the shed toward the barn. At the edge of the yard, he stops, loads the big twelve-gauge, and leans it carefully against a fence post. He disappears into the barn.

When the first two come out, they can barely walk. He is pulling one that staggers and falls to its knees, wheezing and so thin the heaving of its sides reveals ribs I can count even from this distance. The other is foaming blood, drooling from the effort of walking out of the barn, but it stays on its feet. Their bodies steam with fever. He does it simply. He walks to the post, picks up the gun, releases the safety, moves a few steps closer, lifts the long gun, aims, and pulls the trigger. A tiny adjustment, then he pulls the other trigger. Both animals fall in an odd crumpling motion. The one already on its knees throws its head, then topples. The other falls forward, then to one side. The shots are as they should be, the way a shotgun sounds, but the thunks, the thick weights coming down without life, surprises me.

Even through their sickness, the two cattle he leads out of the barn can smell death. The carcasses are still warm, steaming when he leads the new ones to the fence and ties them. Though they are too weak to run, they swing their heads from side to side, their eyes rolling and dripping, their tongues swollen and protruding. This time, because of the movement of their heads, he has to take a minute to aim, making sure he's sighted between the ears, right at the brainstem. There is the same sound: sharp, small as a star, and loud. Then the thudding deflations.

The last pair fight him and collapse. He shoots them where they have stumbled in the manure. His movements are careful, methodical. Only with the last one do I see that he stops, his shoulders very stooped, and looks at the dead animals. He wipes his mouth with the back of his hand. He leaves the carcasses, carries the gun gently away, and returns with the truck. As he works, I can hear the ruckus in the barns. The remaining cattle are bawling; though they have been too sick to wheeze, they are bawling.

I go back down to the kitchen.

"Did you hear?" she asks. She sees my face. "You watched."

"Yes."

"So did I."

That night, after the grueling morning of pulling away the animals and the afternoon of injecting the ones who might survive, he bathes. We all do, and we dress for Christmas evening. My brothers and I are quiet, having helped load the animals on the vet's truck, which will take them to a state facility for disposal. They cannot be sold for meat because no one knows what the antibiotics might have done to them. They cannot be burned as we would have done in the past. My mother is shocked by the waste and the irreverence.

My father's voice is steady until he gets to the verses about the animals. Then it is as if he sees the words in the way that I have begun to see them, not as individual entities but in whole images. The small animals of humankind and the big animal cows, all gathered around the trough of grass and warmth, breathing. Breathing in a rhythm like dark hills, breathing like prayers that cannot be answered. This time I hear not the glory of angels but the bawling of a herd of sick cows, trapped in the lower barns, singing from the dark.

Water Jugs

We pick cherries in the heat of July, at high summer. As I scramble in the trees, on the ladders, and on the ground where I have spilled the cherries, the dry blossoms fall and get caught in my collar and sleeves, and work down my back. They itch. The dust from the trucks flies up in my face, and the fruit makes my hands and arms sticky. If I wipe my sweat or scratch, the sticky gets wherever I put my hands, the itch gets worse. I learn not to put my hands anywhere I don't want to itch. The worst of it is being in a tree, which should be cool, because it's an orchard. But it's not. An orchard, planted densely and growing big healthy trees, stops a good summer breeze right on the perimeter. Inside an orchard, inside a tree, where the cherries are, where I am, it's hot.

The only real break happens when my mother asks one of us to go back to the house, to the well, to fill the water jugs. She uses this errand as a reward for hard work, and it usually goes to Rick, or even to Marijo, the littlest picker, because they are good, steady workers. I am not.

From the tree, I hear the voices of the Mendozas, the migrant family whom my father has hired this year. The trees have reached maturity, and the crop is now too large for our family to pick the ten acres alone. The Mendozas live in the old one-room schoolhouse, where a large shower and an indoor bathroom were recently installed. I am a little afraid of them. I do not yet identify them as individuals. Instead I apprehend them as a collective, a cluster of understated Spanish voices murmuring through the trees, like shy animals who belong here more than I do. They seem unaware of the heat, unaware of itching. They always wear long-sleeved shirts and long pants, and they rarely seem to sweat. Of the Mendoza family, I know only one by name, Miguel, a slim, dark-haired boy, exactly as tall as I am.

"Pick in your own tree," my mother tells me firmly, knowing my weakness for distraction, but I go to the tree where Miguel is picking or, if my mother is in the orchard, I go to the tree nearest the one his family is picking. Early in the morning I listen to the cherries drop into the empty buckets. The soft thud is a tiny percussion, a heartbeat coming and going in the heat. I think he looks at me sometimes through the laden branches.

I wait for Miguel to speak but he never does, though once I hear him answer his own mother briefly, softly, in Spanish. Another time, as I carry a bucket back to the lugs on the truck, I pass him as we shuffle through fescue and orchard grasses. He smiles and nods, a gesture laced with such politeness that his reserve forever becomes a gauge for something I eventually associate with manners but for which true courtesy is the better description. Shyly, I smile back.

That day the orchard fills with the sound of starlings, their glossy black song scrilling among the branches and down the rows, and the rich drumming as pails full of tart charries pour into the empty lugs on the tailgate of the old Chevy truck. Over the long days that follow, I come to care for Miguel's quiet. When I listen for him, what I hear are the unwords from the rest of the orchard. When I can't manage to pick near his tree, the itching is worse, my day hotter and more miserable. I climb a ladder and sit in the high branches, and I pick so slowly I fill barely a lug throughout the entire morning.

I am in the ladder, having picked across from Miguel's tree for most of the day. I have a full pail of cherries, and as I swing down the steps, moving in mid-air, the old canvas harness, worn from many summers, breaks at the buckle where the snap latches onto the handle of the pail. The cherries tumble down in a bright red waterfall into the sand and grasses. I climb down step-by-step, kneel at the bottom of the ladder, and begin picking them up with sticky fingers that quickly become caked with sand and mud. I am so tired I have forgotten to be embarrassed, forgotten to be ashamed. I do not even realize he is there until his dark hands dart into my vision, lifting the cherries quickly and dropping them back into the bucket. Our hands alternate hovering over the bucket, dropping in the cherries. When we have collected as many as we can, I try to say the one word I think I remember from *I Love Lucy*: "Gra-chi-as."

His mother chuckles softly from a nearby tree. He calls something back to her. I wait, but he turns and moves back into the shadows of branches and fruit.

The next day I come back, this time wearing an old belt around my waist to lace the handle of the bucket. The leather cuts at my waist and pulls against my back as the bucket gets heavier with cherries. At noon I unbuckle the belt and bucket, setting them down under the tree I will begin picking after lunch. I think no one can see, so I lift my shirt, twisting, and touch the raw welts that have begun to rise where the leather rubs against the top of my hips. I walk slowly to the truck where my mother, frowning, divides up bologna sandwiches, carrot sticks, and cake. We pass the water jug, beaded with icy water, from hand to hand, mouth to mouth.

When I return to the tree, the leather belt is gone. In its place a regular canvas shoulder harness rests across the pail. I look around but there is no sound among the trees. Here and there, in the farther rows, I can see the lower torso of some picker or the back of someone's shirt, crossed by the dark harnesses, moving into the thick branches. No one is near, not anyone from my family, not anyone from the Mendozas. Not

Miguel. But out of the quiet I hear the rise of the summer insects, the flies and the bees, the purpose and need in their hum. I say nothing. But all the rest of the day I pull the cherries off the branches as if there was nothing that mattered so much in the world. I pull them off with a fervor and meaning that must get attention.

Late in the afternoon my mother idles the truck through the trees, picking up stacked lugs—checking, always checking, to see that every tree is topped. She sees my loaded lugs under the tree. She looks at me quietly, pulls the empty water jugs from the floor of the truck and hands them to me, saying merely, "Be sure to rinse them out first."

It is magic.

With the plastic milk jugs swinging loose in my arms, I run through the long rows all the way to the house. I stand by the well-pit, where the air comes up from the pump cool as a cave, and breathe in the chill musk of the underground. Here the grass is lushly chilled and matted from the spilled water. I take my shoes off. I listen to the hollow, gurgling sound of the jugs filling. I rinse my face and hands, putting my mouth around the tube of water from the hose for a long time and letting it slosh against my tongue. I stay there until I feel guilty, until my sweat has dried and I have summer on my skin, not in the heat, but in the cool comfort and the honor of the water jugs. I heft them up and into my new arms like babies I will carry back to the still orchards. When this is done, I walk slowly back through the rows and rows of regular trees, letting the gallon orbs slosh against my arms. I walk and walk until I find the one tree. There, as the chosen one, I offer up first to Miguel the cool plastic jug as though it were a goblet of fine wine.

Bees

The honey bees arrive one spring during a lush, blossoming time—a wild swarm on the orchard's edge. At first they light in the big apple tree on the south side of the house, hanging from a branch dotted with pink like a large dusky clump of brown-clotted fruit. We watch them from a distance. We are warned not to throw anything at them—not to annoy them—and we don't. We have all been stung before. We leave them alone though we sometimes sit on the tiny southeast porch and peek around the corner to watch the hive evolve. It is nothing like the neat white hives in the beekeeper's backyard. These are wild bees.

After two days, the bees find the rotted spot at the corner of the porch where the porch fascia meets the house siding—a small, forgotten hole that leads them into the darkness of our uninsulated walls. We watch them disappear in a dark humming line, into the studs of the farmhouse. My father shakes his head, but he values bees. Their work is a boon to every farmer, and he has no time to move them. He lets the hive alone, and in the years that follow, the trees closest to the house on the south slope always bear heaviest of any acre of the orchard. My father tells us they are a wild hive—they are afraid of nothing—part truth, part warning.

In fact, the bees don't mind the noise and activity in the orchard or the house, and once they have settled, the character of the hive seems calm. In summer, after work, we play in the front yard, under the mock

orange bush through which they hurtle like tiny bears. They fly in halt-
ing, circular movements, trundling through everything that has a flower,
and finally, like slow escalators, they rise to the hive at the top of the
porch. They rarely sting us, and in the seven years they live in the house,
they swarm again only once.

That first summer I am so little I don't understand their sound.
Bees work all the time—even in the dark. Behind the curtain of night
birds, summer breezes, the patterings of insects and moths, I hear their
hum like dark cream, but it is so much a part of everything that it seems
like a sound in my body. As one summer follows another, their hum has
the sound of foam, haze, and dozing warmth. There, in the walls, they
purr through the heat waves and storms.

Because of their sound, sleep comes better in summer than in any
of the other seasons.

In later years, as we get to know them, we notice when they begin.
Each April, with the first, false-warm days, the walls begin to breathe.
No one can name it, but then, one morning at breakfast, Tom will say, "I
heard them last night." And we put it together that the bees are awake
again and working.

The pastures of the farm spread out in wide rolling hills with a
long, cool swamp on the eastern border. Of the original 200 acres, little
of this back acreage was actually tillable when I was a child. Much of it
was low wetland. Though it would eventually be tilled, in those early
years the land was full of wild grasses, rough meandering streams, and
reedy wetlands with unpredictable, sucking soil. In these open spaces,
with cattle and dogs and trunks of rotting trees, we construct dams in
the creek and forts in the pines, and we run without any sense at all
through tall mullein and grasses.

We run into wild things.

My father is with us. He is looking for a cow about to birth, and
we are all traipsing with abandon through the pines. We step into the

open fields. Tom runs ahead, swinging his stick through the tops of burdock and sumac, stabbing imaginary snakes in the gravelly soil. I see him in the sunlight, silhouetted in the late afternoon. He stops, looks down. He gestures like he is brushing the front of his tee shirt. He does it again, and then again, with an unnatural quickness. His body jerks into a small dance. He drops the stick. The high whine of his scream comes out of nowhere, the shrillness of a small machine gone awry.

My father stops, then orders "Stay here." He rushes, running to Tom, and the tiny, black, x-shaped wings rise and fall, swirling in the grasses around Tom, around his head, thickening with each second. My father wades into it, pulling off his cap, slapping the air around Tom, calling back to Rick and me, "Run. Run!"

Rick looks at me, "Yellow jackets!" He pivots in his tattered sneakers, and his short legs churn back through the broken grasses.

My father lifts Tom under his arms and runs too, his leather work boots thudding in the soft soil, the black and yellow insects whirring behind him like a thin cloud. Tom is a sack under his arms, his screams broken only by the sound of his gasp each time he is thrown against my father's hip.

My father sees me standing, watching. "Run," he shouts, raising his voice in a way he rarely does, and then I too am running, banging through the scrub and low raspberries, through the grass, over the rise into the woods.

"Only nine bites," my mother says as she dabs the pink calamine onto a still whimpering Tom. "Two on your face, three on your hands, two on your arm, one on your neck, and one on your ankle. Really not so bad, considering how mad a nest can get when it's riled." Over Tom's fading gasps, she looks at the rest of us, gathered around the couch as though it were a deathbed. "That's why you must never bother our bees. They'll be just as mad if you ever do anything to their nest. They can sting you so much, you can die." She lets the drama of the statement sink in then turns back to Tom. "Now these are going to swell and hurt for a while, and you may have fever tonight, but after a while, they should just be itchy." Tom, on hearing the news, bursts into another round of weeping.

Bees. I can't believe it. "Yellow jackets are bees?" I ask. Even Tom stops moaning for a moment to stare and roll his eyes.

"But the nest was in the ground."

"Some bees make their nests in the ground," she says. "Or in a stone pile. Where it suits them." She turns her attention back to Tom. "It's a good thing you've been stung fairly often by our honey bees," she says, wrapping rags soaked in ice-water around Tom's wrist.

"Why?" We are shocked at this contradiction.

"Their sting makes these less powerful. Your body already knows what this is. You won't get sick." We are amazed. Even Patti, toddling on the floor, is muttering in her baby way about the stings.

"Tom could get a hundred stings now and it wouldn't even hurt," Rick claims.

"I wouldn't bet on it," my mother says. She shoos us out the door into the summer evening, Rick trailing.

Rick, who leaves his south bedroom window open and the door shut, who falls asleep in a room buzzing with honey bees. Rick, who through all the summers, in the shuffle of scrapes and cuts, by some freakishness of the fields, rarely gets stung. On a farm, there are so many small wounds, no one really notices which child has what immunities or reactions. Once he is stung by a sweat bee, and his wrist swells for three days; but in the rush of pickle season who can tell if a small boy is stung or bruised or just trying to get out of work. If a hornet stings a toe, who remembers if it was Rick or Tom who experienced the swelling and spiking fever that follow. It goes like that through several summers until the summer when Rick's bedroom window is open, his door is shut, and he is sleeping through the July dawn when the bees swarm. Out of the corner of the porch where they have worked peacefully for so many years, the hive divides, shimmering out in a dusty, buzzing cloud. Many of them swarm thickly through the open window and into the bedroom before the cloud moves on to some wild tree, some quieter place in the swamp.

Rick rolls over in the hot sheets onto a half dozen bees. He tosses, scratching and slapping in his sleep. He wakes to a room with bees crawling over the sills and bees in the curtains and bees on his pillows. He listens to the hum and thinks it is louder than usual, even for a hot day. He opens his eyes and watches the bees teeming in the room. He knows them. These are the bungling insects that get into his cuffs, the ones he must watch for when he walks in a field of tufted knapweed.

He feels a little sick as he lies among the thronging sheets; gradually he realizes he has been stung, maybe more than once. He crawls out of bed, scattering bees onto the floor, brushing some of the frantic, stinging creatures away. Before he is even aware of the bees gathering force against him, he shuffles to the door, slowly opens it, then closes it behind him. He staggers down to the breakfast table, where our mother, the woman who knows there is enough danger and crisis in the world not to invent any—and who therefore has underplayed every catastrophe—drops the basket of wet laundry, scattering clean white sheets onto the unswept floor, and sweeps the silent boy into her arms. She does not say the boy's face is twice its normal size, that his eyes are already nearly shut with swelling, that his heart is racing so fast she can feel it under the damp cotton of his pajamas. She merely runs hard, calling for the truck, for any means to get him away from the bees, to get him where there is an antitoxin for his tight, rasping breath against her neck.

I believe the decision was made this way.

Dr. Verbanic is shaking his head as he returns to the waiting room. "You'll have to keep antitoxins around. He should wear a metal bracelet that says he's allergic." He looks at the slim woman, her thick hair prematurely gray, her pale eyes tired and now swollen. He knows this look, common among the farm people he serves. Too much work, too many children in too short a time, and then that Catholic weakness for taking on guilt.

"He's going to be fine, and with just a few precautions around the hives, he'll be in the fields again before you know it."

She holds her quiet.

He tries again. "There's no way you could have anticipated this."

She stares at him. The silence moves across the room until finally he asks, "Ruth, what is it?"

She looks up at him, "The bees live in our house."

"In your house?"

"In the walls of our house."

After a long pause, he says softly, "Well, you'll have to get rid of them."

The beekeeper lives up the north road in a tiny shack covered with brown asphalt shingles. Behind his home, among the dandelions and crabgrass, the neat box hives sit in rows like miniature white churches. He has red hair and smokes Salems while he works. He rarely wears the heavy, screened clothing that other beekeepers wear, preferring sleeveless cotton tee-shirts with short-sleeved plaid shirts over them, work pants, and boots. He is wiry and so slim he looks elfin. He is chain smoking the day he comes to take the hive. I ask him if he ever gets stung.

"Lots. That's why I don't have any arthritis."

He goes to work, smoking the hive until the bees are stunned and silent. Then he climbs the ladder and, with a black crowbar, begins tearing off the clapboards. We watch him from far back under the silver maple. Each time he yanks down a board the squeal of the wood is like a knife. He pulls off another and another.

"God, this thing is big," he says, passing the clapboard down to my father. Each time he pulls a board away, he reveals more comb, more of the dark-clotted, yellow-dotted comb. "And old. Black honey means it's been there a long time." Our honey is black, stormy gray, dark brown, and golden brown. Two, four, eight feet down from the eaves, and two, then three studs to the side of the porch. I imagine it going on forever, going on into all the walls of our house, circling us, this massive, dark-combed, aged honey.

When he climbs down, he nods his head. "Rich hive."

His words clink together like pocket change, laced with greed.

My dad and the beekeeper talk, scuffling their boots in the grass under the porch. The small negotiations move back and forth in understated tones. When he climbs back up the ladder, he works more carefully. After he has identified where the queen is and where the drones are, he leaves that section alone. He begins to pry out the old combs with a wide paint scraper and a small shovel. The combs are like the topographical maps I have begun to study in geography—brown, irregularly shaped continents clinging to the inner lath of our house. I see them as islands on a wall, like maps in school. Without ceremony, he drops these dark masses into a wheelbarrow sitting under the eaves of the porch. He breaks off and pulls down the chunks, dropping them, one after another, into the shallow basin. By the time he finishes, the wheelbarrow is overflowing. Then he spends an hour climbing up and down the ladder, carefully tacking each piece of clapboards back into place.

"I'll be back in a week or so," he says. Leaving the wheelbarrow and its contents behind, he packs his things and drives away, the smoke of his Salems lingering in the spirea. I move closer to the wheelbarrow. At first I am unsure how it is to be done.

I see the bees return and discover the disaster.

But they view it as lush work. They gather on the old combs in the barrow until they resemble a dense, woolen blanket. They cover it with their round bodies, waddle over it, cake it with their warm fuzz, and then, having laid their claim, they begin working it. They work it and work it until they take it back. Through it all, their sound is fierce. They have never been so loud. At night now, the hum enters our muscles, the hollows of our bones where our marrow is held thick as old honey.

I sleep like the peaceful dead. It takes the bees ten days. When they are done, the wheelbarrow is not even sticky.

Only when I run my finger along the edge and stick it into my mouth do I taste anything like the sweetness that belongs where so much sweetness has been. I look at this thing that was full and now see emptiness, and I look back at the chipped clapboards of the house.

The day the beekeeper returns, he is smoking and his hands are nervous. This time he brings a square white box with a black cover. He climbs the ladder and opens one part of the clapboard, the place he left untouched the first time. Working very gently, he removes the queen of this wealthy hive and as many as he can of the bees close to her. He takes the combs in which she and the workers live, then places them into the square, slatted box. He waits and lets the bees find her and gather around her; he puts his hand inside the box, and they cover it with bee fur.

"That means they're safe," he announces to us. I listen to their hum. When he puts the cover on, they become mute. He closes the box and carries it to the open trunk of his car.

When this is done, he and my father open the side of the house again. My mother is there now. On the railing of the porch she has spread newspaper and dozens of sterilized Mason jars. The two men pull off the boards. What the walls reveal this time is pale blonde, nearly perfect, viscous. New honey. It shines. A few bees buzz frantically around their heads, but the men pull the combs carefully away from the inside lath of the house, picking out bits of plaster that cling to the new clumps. They pass these down to my mother, who, standing in the shade on the porch, packs them into the jars, wipes the jars clean of stickiness, and seals them.

Once they hand down a comb dripping with nearly clear syrup. "Nectar honey. It's sweeter," the beekeeper says. "It's off the top of the hive. Got more moisture and floral residue in it."

She calls us to her, and we come like puppies to the teat. She cuts the comb into sections and hands us each a piece. It drips as we lift it to our mouths. The rich amber taste floods my cheeks, and as I suck I wonder what I am tasting. With each lick, it occurs to me that when they took down the honey, we could tell how old it was by the darkness of the combs, but now, all the years are just the same—the year Tom ruptured his spleen, or when Mike died, or the year we learned to swim. Was I tasting the year of the bumper cherry crop or the year the apples froze? The year of my first communion? I know all the summer times I have lived are blurred together now, running into one comb after another. And what is it we suck when we suck this nectar, this honey from the top, this jelly of growing?

Later the beekeeper stops by to tell my dad, "Best working hive I ever seen." The nearly thirty quarts of honey from the hive sweeten our cereal and coffee for three years.

But for the rest of the summer, I sleep restlessly. I toss, longing for their hum. I have no words for why I wake at night or for why the dark feels sharper, the nights cooler, the leaves in the silver maple more shrill. The house is quiet, but sometimes I wake in the dark, hearing one-by-one the soft plunk as the last of the stray bees die in the hollow walls.

The Return

The winter we move into the town of Hart, I am in third grade. The first, and for a long time the only, symptom of illness is that I become progressively quieter. My mother touches my forehead with her knotty hand, looking out at streets as foreign to her as money. She finally calls Dr. Verbanic, who comes to the house at dusk on a damp January evening. He finds nothing wrong but politely asks if our family has moved into town permanently.

"No, we're still in Crystal Valley," my mother responds.

"That's what I thought. What are you doing here?"

"Just for the winter." She is nervous about revealing personal information.

"Why's that?"

"John can carpool to the Du Pont plant from here."

"He's working in Montague?"

"This winter."

"Long drive. I thought you were farming."

"We are. We just. . . . We'll go back come spring."

"And your kids are growing up out there?"

"Yes."

Turning to me, he asks, "What do you miss?"

I'm surprised he asks me a question at all. We are trained to be quiet and listen. It's becoming habitual, though once I talked to everyone, everything.

"Running."

Moving through air like a small balsa plane, my body trilling with the motion of leaves falling, catching the updraft by the barn, whirling among stone piles. And at night, when no one is allowed to have light, holding a flashlight, shining it out the window, into the orchard trees that stand like people in rows to the top of the hill, as though each tree would take off up into the air, tumbling into the wind like angels, like the bodies of something too beautiful to behold, something so dark and good it must be a sin.

Following the second visit with the doctor, I fail the long division test at the new school, and I can't understand how to copy the poem from the board onto the page because there is never enough room for the whole line. My copied words run down the side of the paper like rain running off the roofs of every building that wet winter.

He asks, "What does she do when she plays?"

No one can answer, not even my brothers, who walk to and from school with me every day. Not even me. I cannot remember what I do except for the tests at school, the long division of numbers, and words on their sides, running down the page. Except sometimes the sounds remind me . . . *of the voice in a crab apple tree, its leaves talking differently from those of all other trees, or popple rustling, or the pines' moan* . . . but no, that sound wouldn't be like the pines at all, instead like the train that runs on the tracks across the street, metal's old whine.

By his third visit I am nearly mute, nauseous with a feeling like bricks in my stomach, my skin like a clammy wind. My body aches because just that day the boys have broken their word while I was supposed to be watching them. They had slid off the street like ferrets, down the town's steep river bank, skittered like dark wild stones onto the gray ice, onto and across the forbidden river. Though my feet were wet in my brown shoes, I was filled with the same sharp longing to fly onto the ice, and that one bit of memory, spreading . . . *the old yard light out onto ice so thick on our yard that we skated on it in our shoes until we could not feel our feet but floated, small bodies inches above iced grass, slinging away into air with the lives of all the things that lived on the farm rising with us in some. . . .*

And then I am running down the gray street, running away from my brothers, from their danger and rebellion, telling on them. I cry when, after they are spanked, they turn on me, "Tattletale, tattletale." And then there is the fact that no one will talk to me about words shaping in my mind, about what it is I see, how I see. I never feel I belong.

Looking at my mother steadily, the doctor says "I don't know. If I were you, I'd take her home."

There will be no water for days because the pipes were drained before we moved into town, and the house will be cold because the wood supply is wet, and when we pile out of the Nash with our boxes and trudge under the yard light, there is only a late skim of snow to greet us. But my mother shoves fuses into sockets, gropes for switches, finds pans that smell of chicken fat, heats plain soup.

The lethargy that all winter has forced me into a mute sprawl on the couch, that has silenced the thousand voices in my head, turns feral. My nose runs and drips. Without asking my mother if I can go, I skitter into the barn. *Having wakened into wind that has splintered wild grass on twenty-seven hills, I call the names of stars and a dozen barn cats. Having wakened into the sharp arrow of the yard light splaying away from its tin hood, piercing me, entering my skin and mouth; having wakened among singing trees, among all the angels I know, I begin to run. Run. Run.*

When I finally answer my mother's call and careen into the kitchen, chattering to twenty imaginary friends, my mother, reaching out to grab my chin, gasps at the color in my face, at the sound of my airy giggling.

Not yet, my body has said. Even if I am able to leave, I will have to come back. Over and over, it will be as though I am learning long division or writing a poem that is not my own or trying to cross a river I have been forbidden to cross. No one teaches me how to live without the fields, and so I have to return, wanting both their detachment and the way they stir my growing imagination.

Tractor

The secondhand Allis Chalmers tractor putts slowly down the rows and over the wide, rolling hills of the fields, always pulling something: a mechanical rider, a plow, a wagon, a sprayer, or a manure spreader. It moves over fields like a giant wood borer, working the pulp of its host. Year after year I watch it thud slowly, implacably ahead, the monster wheels with the deep black treads turning in mud or sand or furrows of clay. I watch my father driving this machine, looking like a man in charge. I watch his big hand turn the key in the engine over and over again. I watch him twist the heavy black steering wheel from wet season to dry season, from planting to tilling under. The machine moves, and he knows how to make it move.

My brothers begin riding with him before they are six, first sitting on his knees then standing precariously between his legs. I watch them place their fingers on the wheel; he places his hands over theirs, and they begin to steer the tractor. They learn to shift and brake, and finally to turn the key and drive it themselves. Always, I want to drive the tractor. But when I ride, I stand on the running board to the side of the steering apparatus. I am never invited to take the wheel, though sometimes, while my father is in the kitchen taking a mid-morning coffee and the tractor sits on the edge of the yard, next to the old red gas tank, I climb up onto the tractor, plunk myself into the great iron seat padded with burlap bags, and pretend to drive, yanking the wheel back and forth in a wild, imagined ride.

From the sound alone, I understand the tractor's power, its centeredness on the farm. The sound of its engine is unmuffled, huge and raw. I am afraid of and fascinated by its mammoth gurgle, its crackling backfire. I am afraid of its wheels, afraid of the way it crushes and tears dirt, afraid even of the tracks it leaves in the mud. They are a perfect cast of its power.

I want to drive the tractor. As soon as they are able, *the boys* are encouraged to drive—at first around the barnyards, then around the gray two-tracks in the orchards. Finally they are permitted to drive, slowly, around the asparagus field, pulling the mechanical picker—the winged contraption on which we sit day after day— harvesting the slim green stalks. Driving the tractor seems an honor to me, a way to be nearer the sky and air, to see that everyone else is doing what needs to be done. Driving the tractor is a subtle way of being in charge, not just watching little kids or doing chores but, for hours on end, a job of importance.

I know the requirements: the driver must keep the tractor moving straight down the rows, but slowly enough so that the pickers can keep up. The driver must not let the tractor swerve over the delicate spears; he must pull the picker round after round (once to the end of the row and back) in perfect monotony. The driver must steer the tractor in careful swaths of three, five, or even seven rows, depending on the number of pickers and the makeshift machine. Driving seems like important work, more important than picking, and certainly not without risks. At the end of the rows, the trick is to turn the tractor tightly, without jackknifing onto the picker. This must be done slowly, with a little braking, sometimes by downshifting. I watch the boys get better at it each year. I sit on the rider and break a stalk of good asparagus into many small pieces.

But I always pick. From the earliest times I am a picker, not a driver. My brothers are drivers. As soon as they are able, perhaps by the time they are nine and ten, my brothers are taking turns driving the tractor in the asparagus fields, freeing my mother to pick or haul and my father to work other fields. I want to drive. It becomes a way of determining who I am on that farm. Though early in her marriage and youth, my mother drove tractor, we girls never do. Questioning why this rule and no other separates us from my brothers, I sense now that it has to do with my brothers loving that tractor, being as fascinated with its power as I was, fascinated enough to protect their inherited right to it.

My brothers and I are crowded like beans in a freezer box into the cab of the secondhand blue Chevy pickup my father has recently purchased. This truck is fine—no duct tape on its seats, no rust on its fenders, no dings. We have even washed it a couple of times, unheard of behavior on a farm. Tom is begging to drive this new pickup.

"I can work these gears. Look, I know how you pull it down while you step on the clutch." Rick is watching Tom's hands avidly. The boys will be competitive in whatever endeavor they tackle.

Dad sighs. "Maybe. Maybe after it's loaded, you can drive it back to the house."

I see a small opening and decide to take advantage of it. "If he can drive the pickup, I could drive the tractor while he's doing that."

Both boys turn to me. There is a moment of silence. Dad says nothing.

"You don't know how," Rick says.

"I been watching," I say with more confidence than I feel. "And you can tell me, give me tips, and I'll do it."

"Nah," Tom says. "Rick can drive while I'm driving the truck."

"But I do know. Some. I know how you brake, and how you push in the clutch, and it's got a low and a high gear, and you use the low gear in the asparagus fields."

"You got to know more than that," Rick says.

"And you line up the exhaust pipe in the front with the end of the row, way down the field, and that helps you keep the wheels in the right place." I've heard them discuss this.

My father still has said nothing.

"What about the turns?" Tom asks.

"Yeah, what about the turns?" Rick chimes in.

"I've watched," I claim, but I know this is lame. Even with all their experience, they sometimes misjudge and catch one of the trusses on the wheels. Then the picker leaps and jerks, and if it gets too far into the jackknife, the girder will bend or break.

"Takes more than that," Tom says, adding authority to his voice, shaking his head, and looking at Dad sideways. Still my father does not speak.

"Well, maybe you could show me." I think I am being reasonable. "Let me ride a couple of rounds with you so I can learn, then there'd be more of us who could do that job."

"There's no room up there," Rick says. He's probably right. The driver has to be able to turn freely, looking ahead and back, checking speed against the heaviness of this particular picking and whether the workers are keeping up.

We pull up to the rider, spread like a skeletal bird on the field. Dust flies around it. The Martinez family, the new migrant family with us this spring, is there, waiting. Bushel-sized crates have been spread out over the rider. As we climb out of the pickup, I catch my dad's sleeve. "Can I drive tractor?" He looks at me. "Please, Dad?" The boys stop, looking back.

He sighs, runs his hand over his mouth a couple of times. "Maybe," he says, then nods. "Yeah, you can give it a try."

"When?" I ask, not to be forgotten. He is walking away, and I follow his loping steps almost at a run. "When, Dad?"

He stops, hesitates, then moves on, talking over his shoulder. "Why don't you watch this morning, ask your questions, try it this afternoon."

He tosses this back easily, already moving among his workers, a man in charge.

I am thrilled. I turn to pull crates off the tailgate. My brothers are standing there, staring, appalled.

To their credit, my brothers answer every question I ask. *This is how you slow down, this is how you turn at the end of the round so it doesn't damage the picker, this is what you do if you get off track, this is what you do to stop.* They are already taller than I am, and in order to press down on the brakes, I have to stretch my legs and lift my body as I do when I ride a bike, but I can reach them. I can make the tractor stop.

Then it is afternoon, after lunch, and I am standing in the rough to the side, waiting to drive the tractor. The boys watch me, scuffing, and my little sister, Marijo, piles extra crates on the back of the rider. Then, as the Martinez family slowly empties half-filled bushels and lingers, smoking alongside the rider, Tom starts the tractor with a big roar of the engine. He turns it down to the idling range and pulls it into place. He swings his long legs over the seat, stands on the running board, then jumps. I climb up from behind the tractor, from the more vulnerable place between the tractor and the picker. He doesn't say a word. He walks back to the picker, kicking dirt, and takes a seat next to Rick.

I climb up and take the burlap-covered seat, telling myself to look as though I do this every day. But when I turn around to see that everyone is safely settled, I notice how high this place feels, this seat; and as the workers look back at me, each shows a similar look of surprise, as though they have just seen an animal they didn't believe existed. I turn away from them and let out the clutch. The tractor jerks like something bitten. I push the clutch back quickly, then ease it toward me again more slowly. I pull it into low, and the tractor moves out steadily.

In the first round, I do everything wrong. I try to line up the exhaust pipe on the hood with the end of the row but it seems too wide a measure, and the tractor weaves back and forth, wavering as I overadjust the wheel. At the end of the round, I try to make the turn, but it is almost immediately too sharp. I catch the tires on the girder and have to stop and back up, then start around again. I make a too-wide turn, too many rows over, and it takes me a hundred feet to get us back on the right row. My brothers keep yelling *Get over. Get over.* I think maybe this is too hard, but then I think of giving up the wheel and sitting forever behind the tractor, behind this machine that calls louder than any other on the farm. My face blazes bright red, but I stay put.

This time, as the end of the rows comes in sight, I realize the south edge of the field borders the orchard, so the turn will have to be exquisitely tight or the far side of the picker will swing into the orchard and we will hit a cherry tree. As the end of the rows approach, I veer a little to the right in order to make a wide left turn and watch constantly, looking back and forth until my neck hurts. This time I make the turn, but as I do, the Martinez boy, riding the seat closest to the orchard trees, bolts off the back of the rider and rolls in the dirt as I drag the picker through low branches, scraping a tiny patch of bark off the side of one cherry tree. Tom leaps up, jumps on the tongue of the tractor, and climbs up.

"OK, I'll take over now."

I recognize his confident air and hear his bigger voice rising from his throat. He knows how to do this. "No," I say. "I'm going to finish the field."

"You almost took that tree out."

"No, I didn't," I say. "I just need a little more practice."

I know he wants to take the wheel, to have his place back, and I have given him plenty of reason to do so. I know my hands are sweating, my heart is beating hard, and I feel a little sick. I say again, "No. I'm driving."

Tom shakes his head and stays next to me. I start idling the engine, push the gear into low, and the tractor moves ahead. He turns while it is moving, jumps off, and returns to his place. I pay no attention to him, but concentrate hard on what I am trying to do. I glance back and see the row of workers, settled into the task of reaching down and breaking off the spears as they lurch slowly over the rows.

Even over the low thud of the Chalmers, I can hear the high snap of asparagus spears as the workers break them off at the surface of the soil, a tiny percussion against the heavy engine, a rhythm of light sound against dark. For the first time, I look around, past the rows and rows of asparagus. I can see all over this forty acres and further, past the edge of the field to the swamp and pond on the south, all the way over the pasture to the cedars on the east, up the orchard hill to the north, beyond the road and cornfield to the west. From up there on the seat of the tractor I can feel how much space this property covers, how the land rolls, and how the contours control the soils: sand on the hilltops, gravel in the troughs, clay on certain slopes and lowlands, rocks on anything that was once a ridge. Now, above the low dust rising from the wheels, I can see the weather, a front coming across the western horizon, and I realize this is how my father can tell when it will storm, when he must push us to pick faster. I can feel the wind shift. It dries my skin and lifts the tangled mop of pale hair off my forehead. I watch the exhaust pipe and make the adjustments to the wheel smaller. All the way down the row I am aware of how big the field is, how big the farm is, how it seems to go on and on to some distant boundary that in turn blurs into the other distant farms around us—Uncle Joe's and Uncle Butler's and Smith's and Birkman's and all of them with tractors working their fields. It is spring, and the light soil shows off wide patches of green: corn and wheat and hay and fields with seedlings of cucumbers or zucchini. I know I am seeing something so beautiful that it is hard to look at it and take it all in.

I drive the tractor out and over this land, and as I do, it steadies me in a way I have wanted to know. When I come to the end of the row, I am cooler and able to make the turn. I see my brothers shake their heads—not a perfect turn, so they cannot give way—but Marijo grins and ducks her head to me, and I turn back and aim for the other end of the field where there is a low rise before we come down to the end of the row. All the long way back I keep the tractor straight, seeing the rows and the field, feeling the connection to the work, and hearing the dull thud of the engine as a heartbeat like my own, going on and on, rolling some wheel of motion into some future I only begin to sense.

The slope rises more quickly than I imagined it would, and the moment of reverie and wonder passes as we crest this low hill. We are only a few hundred feet from the end of the field. At the very end of the rows, my father, guessing about where we will end up on this round, has parked the new pickup with its huge boxes in the bed so we can empty the crates. He has walked away, to the east end of the field to check for length and bug damage or to take a leak. So he is not watching when, trying carefully to think about the slope and anticipating that we will need to go slower, I stand up and try to reach with my foot and press firmly on what I think is the brake pedal. Instead it is the clutch release. The tractor begins to roll more quickly. I think to myself, *the brake, the brake,* as my foot slips off the clutch and catches between the two pedals. I am watching my foot, not the field, trying to pull the shoe up through the gap, and the tractor is moving faster than it has all day. In that sudden place where nothing makes sense, I grab the hand clutch and thrust the engine into high, thinking, *the brake, the brake*. Then Tom is yelling, *Stop the goddamned tractor*. I hear Rick shouting, *S*hit, *shit, oh shit*. And there are sharp Spanish words I have never heard before punctuating the air. I look back to tell them it will be just a sec—my foot is caught—but I never say it. Instead I see my little sister, Marijo, her mouth open wide and her arms reaching up to cover her head.

The tractor, moving through an out-of-control turn, hits the pickup truck squarely in the bed and rear fender, pushing it unsteadily ahead a few feet and crumpling the metal as it does. The impact is not a single one but a series of small impacts, grinding stops and starts, a sequence of fitful jerks and bumps. The two metal objects screech out a set of sharp metallic clanks, coupled with the cacophony of panicked human language. Finally, as my foot comes loose, the machine dies in its tracks with a last backfire: a loud shot together with a puff of gray smoke punking out of the exhaust pipe. All I know is the crumpled truck, and a babble of angry and frightened voices. I jump and hit the ground, then I am running, running, running.

High in the hay mows of the big barn it is dry, dusty, and silent. I sob into the sleeve of my shirt. I know the barn's offering of safety is illusory. I cry deeply, my face pressed into the rough bales, knowing that the truck is wrecked, that I have killed someone and hurt many, and that I can never, never go back to them.

My father comes quietly, climbing slowly over the great mows. He lies down on his side next to me, bracing his head with one hand. After a while, with the other, he rubs my back between the shoulder blades. His big palm, gently circling and circling, brings me slowly down from the high, dramatic, and deathlike place where I was headed. Finally I turn toward him. As we have all through my little girl years, he rolls onto his back, and I curl close into his shoulder. He stares up into the rafters, into the dark, marred ten-by-ten beams, as though he were reading them. After a while, I lift my head, and the tears come new. I choke, "You better tell me who's dead."

He turns his head and looks at me sharply. He does not smile but answers quietly, "No one's dead."

My breathing is out of control for several minutes as the gasping breaths rack through me like a flooded spring creek. But I believe him. "And hurt?"

"No one's hurt. Just scared. And mad."

After this settles in, I feel a fragile calm. I nod slowly. "I'll have to buy you a new truck. You can have all my savings, and I'll work the rest of my life. . . ."

"Truck's running. Didn't bend the frame or break the axle."

"But I saw the crash. The side was all crumpled in and the back broken. . . ."

He sighs. "The tailgate will never be the same."

I stutter. "It's running?"

He nods, "We might bang out the side after a while. Still carries a load. All that counts." He looks back up at the beams.

I stare, tears still streaming, at this man who is telling me lies. In that place where I have begun to see what love might be, I see that he is lying to me to make the pain ease up, that the lie is going to be the way I will be able to go back.

"I'll pay for everything, Dad. To get it fixed, to straighten the side. I'll make up for this."

"Make up for what?" he asks, speaking to the dark air above us in the rafters.

I take a deep breath. It comes out so ragged and strange I feel like some other being made the sound. "I couldn't drive tractor."

There is a long pause. Here he cannot lie. "Nope. Probly best you didn't try again."

There is no comfort for it.

After a while he sits up, pulls me into a rough hug, and says, "Come on back when you're ready."

As he starts to climb down, I am coming back into myself. So I ask the question: "Will you tell the boys not to pick on me?"

There is no hesitation. "Yup." And he is gone. Though as I sit, sniffling, I realize his promise will do little good.

I stay there for a long time. It is a new pain, mixed with the relief that I have not hurt or killed someone, the strange sense of luck that the truck still runs and that I have been saved from something so laced with terror that my skin feels tender everywhere. But behind that relief and luck is sadness. For a long time I am so surprised by it that I think it is physical, and I touch my body to see if I am injured. But this is not about bones and flesh. There in the barn this slow ache moves through my cells. It does not leave me. It is as though it has always been there. I know it will never leave.

I have lost the chance to be one of them.

I will never drive tractor. I will never be a farmer. Eventually I will get up, walk out of the barn and down to the house and into the fields again. I will do the work, though less and less willingly. I will always be listening, but I will never feel the power over the fields, over life, which for one brief moment, driving tractor, I did have.

The Witness

In the farmhouse where I grow up, the oak table, a rich golden oval on a single pedestal, becomes over time the only object that knows. Like many old things in old houses, it has its own wisdom, its own way. As a result it keeps mostly silent. Balanced evenly, immovably on its forty-inch base, it listens to the raucous exchange of life sweeping among the seven people who come together each day above its quiet. It speaks through touch, a solid thing in contact with elbows. It speaks by offering the even lines of oak grain at which I stare when I cannot meet the eyes of the person sitting with me. Its surface never curves. It is level as a table should be—flat, reliable, knowing fear only of great things like fire or rot. It offers a placid center for all the lighter, airy, transcendent voices flying over it.

At dinner we spill on it and pound on it, asking the necessary questions over it. We come to lunch from the asparagus field or cherry orchard dirty and cranky, and we feel the sticky surface of one single note of tiredness as we lean on it. We come to breakfast on cold mornings and hold round bowls of stiff oatmeal against its plane, the roundness of our bodies against the odd horizon a big table makes in a room. We come with mugs of strong, milky coffee, and we trace the surface over and over with our fingertips as babies explore their own mouths.

It is one place where we talk.

This is the place where Dad brings his midnight sandwich, Mom brings mending. I will teach Patti new math at the table, and Marijo will cut the cloth for her wedding dress there. At that table we often cry, leaning into it as though it were a mother, a pillow, a kiss.

Before I leave the farm, I often sit alone there at night. I ache to leave and cannot. I come to this table wanting to know its trust in itself, its quieter base—that though the weight of our world descends on it, it is never destroyed, because our fears are not the great fears.

It is night. The yard light spills in onto the table from the north window. I am sitting, looking out the north window through the yard light, toward the dark fields. I have paper in front of me. I have been try-ing to write something. Marijo pads into the room. She is seven, and her Buffalo Bill pajamas are faded, shiny with wear and way too short for her long legs. She climbs onto a chair near me. She is such a tall girl, and so strong that she is working nearly full days in the fields. We forget that she is still a little girl.

"Whatcha doin?" she asks, needy for attention.

"Nothin'. Go back to bed."

"Will you help me say prayers?"

"You did that already."

"You do it better."

I look at her. She has a beautiful, wide face and my mother's almost auburn hair, but her body is already the body of a farmer, her limbs stur-dy and muscled. She is at that age where anything could happen. I put down the pen and she crawls onto my lap. We sit there together, running our fingers over the grain of the table. She wiggles to see my face.

"Mom says you're going away."

"Maybe."

"To be a nun?"

"I don't know yet. It's an idea."

She sighs. "I don't think you should go."

"I might not."

"But you know," she says, as if considering whether a tomato is ready to pick, "You might like it better."

She leans back and folds her hands.

Sometimes we cannot know ourselves except by the ways in which we differ from the solid places where we began. I am not like the great oak table of my home, but knowing myself has much to do with being different from that oak, from its utter reliability. I want to assume its placidity, its stoic head-on flatness. But on those nights when I sit at the table, staring out at the farm, I learn I can never truly know the house or the farm, not the way my mother and father and siblings do. After many nights there, I understand my place at the table better: I can change nothing of the way my family thinks or how the fields and farm, the planting and harvest, the demands of land touch them. I cannot change one line of the grain, the implacable face of the table.

But I can lean on the table. I learn that if I lean hard enough, it will give a little; just the push, and it will tip in my direction. That is all. It feels my weight, nothing more. This nearly imperceptible acknowledgment of me makes me think that if I were there now, I would lean down and carve my name in it.

The Host

I am standing in a line of girls in the blue-and-gold chapel of Marywood Academy—the motherhouse for the order of the Roman Catholic Dominican sisters—standing at six in the morning with a hundred high school girls. We are all dressed in royal blue blazers, white blouses, and pleated plaid skirts, with royal blue beanies bobby-pinned to our heads. The beanies have the *Veritas* shield embossed in gold and royal blue on the front. It reminds me of a third eye floating above our bangs and brows.

The communion line moves slowly forward, toward the priest dressed in white robes and the traditional vestments of daily mass. As each girl reaches the front of the line, she raises her head, tips back her chin, and shoves her tongue out of her mouth to receive the host. There is something mechanical and doll-like about the gesture. The priest murmurs in Latin and places the host on her tongue; the girl closes her mouth, turns, and walks down the side aisle, back to her place in her pew, and the next girl moves into place. In line, a few yawn, a few hold their rosaries as they wait, a few have hymnals in their hands. From these they read the daily liturgies.

I fold my hands and bow my head, moving forward with the line. I am so sleepy. The only thing keeping me awake is being on my feet, and now the smells from the big kitchen, located on the ground floor directly below the chapel, waft up to us. The scent of toast and eggs mixes with the scent of stale incense from Sunday's high mass. My stomach growls so loudly Sister Maryann turns in her pew next to the head of the line and looks at me over the top of her thick glasses.

It is my turn. I step forward so that I am standing directly in front of the priest. I raise my head, lift my chin, and stick out my tongue. He places the host on my tongue, but as I pull it back into my mouth, it catches on the edge of my upper teeth. Instead of being taken into my mouth—where it would disintegrate into tiny, tasteless fragments—it slips off the tip of my tongue and drops straight down, a pale circle with the small weight of a coin, onto the terrazzo floor.

I gasp, suddenly awake but stunned, frozen, aware the line is not moving, that the white polka-dot of the Body of Christ has dropped to the floor at my feet, spittle shining on one edge. Everything around me is still. Without thinking, I bend down to pick it up. It is habit, a gesture of good manners to pick up the thing one has dropped. I swear I would have put it into my mouth. I swear I would have been reverent. But the priest's arm, draped with the white sleeve, springs toward me like a snake, grabs my wrist, and holds back the hand that is doing what it is supposed to do.

The priest has never touched me before, and rarely has any one touched me with such rude strength. I am like a small rabbit, half crouched, my hand reaching, poised. But his hand has a grip that stops my motion. While I squat at his feet, he reaches with his other hand, picks the damp host off the floor, and puts it in his own mouth. I look up at him. He is frowning, red-faced, clearly shaken. He stands, takes another host from the chalice, holds it before me, and murmurs darkly in Latin. I rise, so muddled I do not know what to do until Mary Alice, the senior standing behind me, nudges me. Then I raise my head, open my mouth, and stick my tongue out as far as I can. He places the host on my tongue with an unfamiliar firmness, as though he is making sure it will stick, and I close my mouth. As I turn to go, I cannot stop myself from glancing at the church full of nuns and girls. Every student, with her royal blue and gold beanie blazing above her eyes, and every nun from young to old is staring at me.

Until that moment I still believed I might become a bride of Christ. I might take the habit. I might wear the penguin-like but deeply revered black-and-white habit of the Sisters of Saint Dominic. I thought I might find God here in this stone place because I had begun to realize that the fields would be too hard for me to follow.

I am here as a freshman in high school, and though I miss the farm, the sounds of my family, the lofty, dark barns, I want to stay. When I am awake at night, I miss the wind, the tree outside my window, and the stars across the winter sky. I miss the animals and even my brothers. I miss my little sisters and my mother, my father's quiet steadiness. But I believe I am meant to be here, and that maybe I will become a nun. I am happy to be in this place of big sweeping lawns and wide halls, where everything seems majestic and orderly. I am just thirteen.

Marywood sits high on a long slope on the east side of Grand Rapids, a thriving city two hours south and east of the farm in Oceana County. The convent is a massive, u-shaped stone building, surrounded by graceful trees and elegant lawns sloping down to a creek with a grotto dedicated to Mary. The wing to the east holds the academy, the boarding school of the convent, where both traditional boarding students and the high school aspirants are taught and housed. On the first floor there is a large and beautifully appointed chapel open to the public, as well as the administrative offices of the academy. Down a wide, tiled hall is a spacious room where the nuns and their families can meet, and where occasionally, with reserve and ceremony, receptions are held.

This meeting room is called the Madonna Lounge. No one ever thinks about or laughs at this name. It is always said with reverence. The room is named after the hundreds of Madonnas housed there. It is a classic space, with the kind of furniture on which no one sits for very long, where all the couches and tables, the wing chairs and heavy end tables are placed to invite the contemplation of the Madonnas, perched in perfect rows in the display cases, on shelves, pedestals, small tables. The Madonnas come from all over the world: brightly garbed Spanish Madonnas, hand-carved Indian Madonnas, glittering Madonnas from Thailand, an ebony Madonna from Africa. Wherever the Dominican sisters have gone, they have brought back Madonnas, often made by converts and the people the mission serves. They set them in this room, where the repeated image of this one woman, Mary—the female pivot of the Roman Catholic Church—becomes so multiplied and varied that the room resembles a doll collection in a museum.

I remember the faces of Mary. Usually they are looking down at the child, always a child of perfect proportions. But sometimes Mary is looking up, in the way someone gazes when trying to remember something. Perhaps she is looking to the heavens, offering the child to God. I walk around the room, absorbing its contradictions and abundance. In my imagination, the Madonnas look down at me, and I pretend that at any moment they will speak to me.

Unless there is some sign, like bad weather on the farm, I suspect I am meant to stay, to be among the sisters. I hope to live among the holy Madonnas, and so I look at them. Some are friendly, some haughty. They become important to me—not because I worship them but because I make them alive. I love Mary. No matter what culture or race makes her, she is girl-like. Not a woman but a beautiful girl. I want to be as beautiful as she is. I envy the perfect skin, the flowing robes, the look of admirable saintliness on her face. In the early weeks at Marywood I find the Madonnas comforting. Though I am still filled with awe at the variety of her images, I give each one a different personality: this one with the gold-trimmed shawl is arrogant, this one with the red veil is friendly—

though one must get to know her first. The brown one in the silver sarong is shy.

During the time I am getting to know the Madonnas, I am invited by Mary Alice to participate in a fund-raiser for the missions. Students are asked to serve as ushers on Sunday afternoons in a new, downtown movie house, the Savoy. Our wages are given to the Dominican missions. I sign up for *The Sound of Music* and usher at two shows on each of three Sundays. I love the film, learn it by heart, and mouth all of Julie Andrews' lines. She is another version of the Madonna, lovely though not as pure. I also love the theater: its buttery popcorn smell, its dry, silvery air, even its patterned carpet stained with Coke. The marquee makes me feel jumpy inside. And the clothing of the families who come to the theater in their Sunday best is fashionable and more tailored than any I have ever seen. I feel awkward and clumsy in my uniform, even if I roll up the waistband as I have seen the older girls do.

One Sunday, after the second show has begun, I am sitting near the end of a row toward the back so I can help any latecomers to their seats down front. A woman enters. She is dressed in black. I only notice her because I hear her heels clicking on the tiled floors of the foyer. When I get up to assist her, the big mountain scene rolls across the screen. As Julie Andrews declares that she will go to the hills, the woman is silhouetted in the Alpine light, one hip cocked like a rifle. Her face is turned sideways. She has red hair swept high on her head, heavy eyeliner like Cher, thick lips, and dark lipstick. She wears a tight turtleneck sweater. I notice she has big breasts. Her skirt is black, the shortest I have ever seen. She wears a kind of hosiery I have never seen before, black with patterned holes. I hesitate, then go up to her and whisper.

"May I have your ticket, please."

"Don't have one."

"I can't seat you without a ticket."

"I'm going to sit with the manager."

"Oh," I say stupidly. I'm not sure what to do with this information but the manager, a swarthy, overweight man, appears and nods to me. "It's OK."

They sit down together in the last row, seats which are never occupied unless the theater is sold out because, the manager has explained, "the sight lines are bad." I turn away, giving myself over to the perfect magic of Maria's mishaps. The show runs through its repertoire, and I am lost in "Favorite Things," "Do-Re-Mi," "I Am Sixteen," and a half dozen other examples of perfect family entertainment.

Halfway through "I Must Have Done Something Good," I hear a soft moan. At first, because I am involved in the show and because I don't know this sound, it is like white noise. But when I hear a gasp loud enough to break my concentration on the film, I turn around. In the light from the screen, I see the manager leaning back, his eyes closed. He is breathing heavily, and his arms are holding something on his lap. The woman is not visible, and I wonder where she went. Then I think perhaps he is sick, perhaps he is having a heart attack. I start to get up.

The woman lifts her head from his lap. In the dim light I see her wipe her mouth and turn toward the screen. She catches my glance. She looks at me haughtily and snickers. I look past her to the man, who is wiggling now. He stops and looks at her. He reminds me of a hunting dog, all longing with big ears. She turns to him, her head tilted back, her shoulders rolling toward him. She whispers low. He nods, then she disappears again. He sees me staring. "Turn around," he whispers hoarsely.

One rainy Saturday in October I walk out to the grotto on the elegantly sloping lawn. There a gray Madonna, made from cast concrete, withstands the weather of every season. This Mary does not hold a child. Her arms are held out as though calling those who come to take her hand. I kneel on the cement kneeler shaped like a small boat and pray that I will find my way into this place of Marys. Praying to be like them, I stay there a long time, unable, after my first impulsive thoughts, to concentrate. I feel out of sorts. I hate my body. I want to be like the Madonnas but I find myself thinking about the woman in the theater. The man. The moaning. I know this has to do with sex. I am not unaware of sex but my experience is with the farm, with breeding, not with my own body, not with what people do. Nor is it like what my parents do, not like the gentle kissing I sometimes hear from their room at night. But I also know there is a relationship between that and my periods, between that and birth. All these things seem secret and sinful, one image running into another, blurring together feelings of curiosity and fear.

I know these are bad thoughts. I kneel until I am soaked, and after I return to the third floor dormitory I am chilled and sick.

In the dormitory, of the two rows with six beds each, I sleep in the back. I have a window at the head of my bed, one of several facing north, so I can rest on my bed, look down over the front lawn, and spy on the comings and goings of the sisters and the priests. The back of the grotto, with its landscaped shrubbery, the distant street, and the curved driveway to the busy street are all in my view. As the weeks pass, my cell, with its white curtains dividing the beds at night, begins to feel like a tower. I am high and separate from the world on the street, or the one I glimpsed at the cinema. Here in the dormitory the nuns talk to us, lead us in prayer, supervise our activities. I am aware of their overseeing. They sometimes have the same distant, untouchable look of the Madonnas. I feel awed and often fearful of them, but I want them to like me. And I want to be like them.

But today Sister Mary Ann, our supervisor, is talking to us from the wide doorway that faces these windows, making announcements for the weekend as we prepare for Friday night supper. I sniffle into a navy, print hanky I brought from the farm. I have a cold and need to rest, but when

I fall asleep I dream of hills, cornfields, asparagus fields. In the dreams everything needs picking. All the harvests are coming at the same time: asparagus, berries, cucumbers, apples, beans—all in the same season.

Sister Mary Ann's words catch my ear.

"Tonight and on future Friday nights, and if—and only if—you have no duties or homework, you will be allowed to watch the new color television from eight until ten o'clock. You must return to the dormitory as soon as your programs are finished."

There is a smattering of approval. Patti Sykes, a girl I know will never be a nun, asks, "Sister, can we watch whatever we want?"

"The sisters and I will review the programming. You may request a show, and we'll preview it."

"Can we watch *Man from U.N.C.L.E.?*"

"We'll see."

Unbelievably, they approve the show.

Gunfire spits across the screen; the man in the suit takes out his ink pen and speaks into it. A helicopter swoops in and picks him up seconds before the evil T.H.R.U.S.H. agents are destroyed by the bomb he has planted. I have never seen characters like these—not in any of my mystery books, not in any of the stories I have read. Illya Kuryakin and Napoleon Solo have a detached toughness, a heroic understatement of ultimate confidence. They are better than the knights in fairy tales, better than the war movies, better even than Maria and Captain von Trapp standing up to the Nazis.

But the Madonnas are also watching. I sit on the finely woven carpet of royal blue and cream. I lean back onto the arm of the formal couch and wrap my arms around my waist. One of the seniors turns off as many lights as she can get away with. The screen tosses its metallic colors over our faces and bodies. Looking modestly down, even the Madonnas seem to glow.

Another fight on the screen, this one in the underground catacombs of some foreign city. Napoleon and Illya dispatch members of the T.H.R.U.S.H. gang with a laser, but not before Napoleon is wounded. He tells Illya and the other agents to leave the flooding compound without him. He will die for his friends—but he never does. There are secrets to be captured. There is almost always a woman to be rescued. They carry her out of the ice chamber seconds before she would be instantly frozen to death, and, of course, she falls in love with Illya.

There in the Madonna Lounge my body feels tight, full of longing, a hunger I have no name for. Everything aches. The air feels different on my skin. I find myself staring at the TV. There they are. And with every nerve in my body fully awake, for the first time I fall in love. Or lust. With hundreds of Madonnas looking on, with my hands wrapped around my waist so tightly they leave marks, my heartbeat accelerates, my face and hands sweat. I lean back into the heavy brocade of the couch, and my imagining is so vivid I can feel his mouth on mine, his hands on my body.

I buy a new black notebook, change my first name from Anne to Anne-Marie because it sounds more European. During religion class I develop and practice a signature with loops. I begin to write stories, stories in which I am always the heroine, the woman who helps them, sometimes saves them, whom Napoleon Solo adores but with whom he can never quite get together. I read some romances and feel the lurches in my stomach as I read the sex scenes.

I sweat, but I am afraid of the couple in the dark.

Yet every Friday night I wait for the television show, restless from supper to prayers to study hall to the few minutes in my cell where I sit with my notebook. At eight o'clock, I am the first down the three flights of terrazzo stairs to turn on the TV. I cannot write during the show itself; I am too obsessed with Napoleon Solo's every move. But while the commercials are on, I make notes, scribbling ideas for the stories I have begun tentatively to write. At first they are just paragraphs describing my favorite scenes in that week's show. Then I rewrite the scenes, casting myself as the main character. As my writing evolves, I begin to invent plots. After watching the show on Friday night, I spend the weekend bent over the library table under the crucifix at the east end of the dormitory, forgetting homework, forgetting laundry, forgetting prayers. As I write, it all becomes true, or at least truer. I believe in the girl in the stories.

The day after the incident of the dropped host I wake at night, restless and sick, to hear the wind blowing. It reminds me of cold nights in my room at home. I get up and creep out of the dormitory, down the stairs to the Madonna Lounge. Gray-green light from the street falls on the Madonnas' faces, holds them in shadows, planes of angled light and dark. I kneel in the middle of the room, my back to the TV, facing the Madonnas who have stared down at every moment of my naive and childlike lust.

"Dearest Mary, Mother of Jesus, I know dropping the host is a sign. Please help me to honor you better. Don't let me write any more stories about kissing Napoleon Solo. I know the stories have impure thoughts. I know I dishonor you and my parents and my teachers when I write them. I'm really sorry. Please help me not to write any more, to dedicate myself to you more fully."

My prayer is desperate. I do not watch *Man from U.N.C.L.E.* that week, and I vow not to go again, but my fantasies grow more vivid. I wake night after night, having dreamt about spies and kisses, all mixed with fields where a woman in black, fishnet stockings laughs at me.

Afternoon religion class is held in a long narrow room crowded with wooden desks, five rows wide, nine rows deep. Forty-five girls gather for the class three times a week. The priest enters the room with big steps, his white robes flapping at his knees, his rosary habitually fingered in his chubby hands. He is a large, pale-faced man, and the gleaming mantle across his shoulders is crisp and wide as a piece of armor. Sister Augustine announces, *Today, Father will teach the class.*

He looks around. He meets my eyes and moves on, surveying the room until he has everyone's attention, and then he begins.

"A few days ago, at morning mass, a very disturbing thing happened. A host was dropped on the floor of the chapel. A blessed host."

The room is silent. The color rises in my face. His voice takes on the tone of an adult being deliberately reasonable. "I know how this happens. The tongue is dry and the body is lazy. You must always make sure your mouth is moist and that you open your mouth far enough and thrust your tongue forward far enough that it is easy to place the host on your tongue."

He pauses. I stare at the map of the ancient world on the wall straight ahead of me, where Mesopotamia is outlined in bright orange.

"You must know, however, that this is the Body of Christ, that it is very wrong to be even accidentally careless of the host, that when we do so we are sinning against the great mysteries, that we cannot ever be too careful of our undisciplined ways. We are all sinners, and we must ask God's forgiveness for our incautious manners. Let us examine other sins of carelessness against the Body of our Dear Lord."

The Tigris and Euphrates rivers are dark lines dividing the valley from the rest of the known world. I watch them all through the hour that his voice drones on and on, discussing the sins of weakness, the sins of oversight and omission, the sins of even accidental touching. I tell myself that someone will save me from this moment, but I know no one will: not any of the girls, not any of the nuns, not even my fantasies. I stare hard at the gray desert between the rivers.

"And just as the host should never touch the floor, or any unblessed surface, so must our bodies be committed to only holy and blessed touch, a touch unsullied by impure thoughts."

Did he know about my stories too? Didn't he know dropping the host was an accident? And how could he connect the dropped host with my impure thoughts? But he did, and of course it was all connected. He had read my secrets.

I spend an hour in the chapel after school, near tears, full of the fear and guilt that only the young can feel, coming at last into a field of emotion with which I am unfamiliar. That night I go down to the Madonna Lounge and watch, with all the passion my young heart can muster, the *Man from U.N.C.L.E.* I give myself over to the fantasy of the protagonists' battles, the microfilmed mystery of lost justice, the quickness of their bodies. When the show is over and every one has drifted out but me, I walk around the room, looking at the Madonnas. Nothing in my strict Catholic upbringing has prepared me for their beauty, their purity. For each one that I can touch, I run my fingers along the bare feet, down the fold of the robe, the perfect hands. They do not respond. They do not forgive. They do nothing.

I open my notebook. I read them a story, and their perfect eyes do not change. I read them another story, and still nothing happens. I read the third story standing up, and as I do, I realize there are some changes I would like to make. It is a story about a windstorm on the sand dunes, and if Napoleon were lost in the storm, and I were to know the secret ways of the sand, then I could rescue him better by bravely leading the way out. Perhaps it would be better if I added some dialogue. I stop and make notes. Another part seems unreal, not described well enough. I am still writing, having forgotten the Madonnas, when Sister Mary Ann finds me and sends me to bed with a sound scolding for missing curfew. The Madonnas look on, perfect and implacable. I visit them all year, wishing I could be like them. They never change.

The first morning I walk back onto the asparagus field, the lessons come back as though *I* had not changed—my hands will bleed from the dry stalks left on the light soil, my skin will become sunburnt, I will wear sleeveless shirts in the morning and long-sleeved ones in the afternoon. I will drink from a plastic jug, dreaming as I work.

One hot June morning I stumble down to the table for breakfast. Crushed strawberries, mounded into a chipped ceramic bowl that belonged to my grandmother, mix with the scent of coffee already an hour on the burner. I pour a cup. My mother looks at me and sighs, wondering again if I am too young to drink coffee. I look at her. She is dressed for field work.

"Which field first?" I ask her.

"South. They'll start at the end by the old schoolhouse."

"How many hours?"

"Looks like all day."

I sit down to the fruit and toast. The table creaks.

"Where's the Penneys' catalog?"

"In the bathroom."

She looks at me. "Why're you drooling over clothes? You just need new blouses for the fall."

I look back. She is silhouetted in the light from the east window, her body moving nervously from sink to oatmeal pan.

"I'd like to try the public high school."

She turns, picks up her cup, looks at me for a long time over her coffee, sighs again, puts the coffee down. Finally she speaks. "It would be cheaper for us." She lifts her head. "But what are you going to do with yourself?"

All summer I work in the fields to make money so that in the fall I can purchase short skirts and those new panty hose for public high school. When I unpack my things in my old bedroom, I stack the black notebooks on the small, built-in desk in the corner of my room. Sometimes I work on them, rereading and adjusting the stories. But as the summer wears on, I write other stories, ones that have nothing to do with spies and lust. Sometimes I write something I think may be a poem. At the dime store, I buy a diary, but it doesn't work. One day never seems to equal one page.

The field is hot. The killdeers screech and play their wounded act whenever the picker rolls close to their nests, but they always return to them. No matter what happens, they go back and find that almost invisible place in the forty-acre field that holds their eggs. When I arrive early in the morning, there is a coolness that will dissipate within an hour. The light is rare, simple and clean. There is clarity, but the dust will rise before we begin. Sometimes I feel outside it all, as though I am watching something I am not a part of. Then our voices seem like the voices of beautiful animals waking, beginning to migrate or forage, the sounds of short exchanges and tender-gruff greetings they would make after rising from their sleeping places.

But most days I feel only the field demanding that we pick this crop.

That summer we cross and recross the fields, not speaking much, saying only the prayer of work. One afternoon my littlest sister, Patti, now seven, crawls up onto the metal rollover pipe strutted over the wheel of the mechanical picker. She balances on the iron bar and squats there watching over us, proud of her eminence. Tom, driving the tractor, is focused ahead, lining up the exhaust pipe with the end of the row to keep the picker straight over the rows. He is not checking on the workers, assuming that by this time of year we can keep up.

No one sees Patti's foot slip down into the open wheel casing. Her light tennis shoe catches between the steel rim and the old rubber wheel. She tries to pull it out, bracing herself, but her denim jeans have gotten caught. I hear her small squeals and turn to see her face squeezed into an expression of astonished terror. I see her leg slipping by inches into the well. She is being trapped in the wheels of the machine, sucked into their inevitable turning. And though I am reaching for her immediately, trying to grab her by the torso, balancing myself on the edge of my seat, trying not to fall into the path myself, I cannot release her. I stand up, braced on the seat of the rider, holding her under her arms, pulling back from the machine.

I scream and scream.

Tom stops the tractor.

While we hold her, while she whimpers and cries out softly, he backs up the rider, and finally it releases her leg, scraped but not broken. She sobs in my mother's arms for whole minutes while we stand around, kicking dirt in the middle of the field, looking at the expanse of long rows still growing before us.

My brother walks up to me. "Why'd you have to scream like that?"

"I didn't think you could hear me."

"We heard you. You didn't have to get so excited." My brothers and I have been close since I returned from Marywood, but now he looks as far away as the horizon.

We climb back on. The tractor putts and roars, and the slow motion begins again. No one speaks to me all afternoon.

They don't understand why I screamed. Even my mother scolds me for overreacting. I keep saying, "She was trapped. She could have been crushed. I had to get your attention." They do not believe me, disturbed as they are by anything that seems overly dramatic. But every time I close my eyes, I see how she could have been killed. I see again the unthinking violence in the machine, the harsh demands of the field.

And yet there is something else, something that, as I grow and change, I will have to learn and relearn. As I pick and lift and pour out a harvest of green, as I sort the rotten cherries from the chilling tanks, hang clothes on a frayed line, watch animals die, as I grope for the words to say what I feel about the mostly silent gods of the fields, I am aware always of an invisible, contradictory love. For despite their utterly implacable surface, I love how these fields make me, how the weight of farm work shapes my being, how the rich liturgy of sounds—including the screams—echoes through the cells of my body even as my brain learns with equal clarity that I cannot belong here. Even as a young girl, I begin to see how the heart-place where love is given but not acknowledged can be the knife-edge of imagination, that very place where identity is caught in the wheel and the wheel turns dangerously and then, miraculously, there are the silent arms that save you.

Pulling Down the Barn

August 1994

I didn't expect it to be so hard. After all, the roof had succumbed to pigeon droppings, wind, and rot a decade ago. But inside, the clear splay of sun falling through the open knots in the pine siding on the west wall came down in that dot-to-dot dance on the floor, and I could still have stepped where those small moons of light landed, still have moved through the pattern I once did every time I entered that cathedral of cows and pain, dust and light.

No one knows anymore how to take a barn apart. This one was put together with ten-by-ten logs thirty-seven feet long, marked by ax blades and pegs the size of hammer handles, all fitted like an ancient puzzle of sticks and space. It should all come apart easily, like an egg with a seam, like the golden marble falling into the center where everything unlocks. But my brothers didn't know. They started pulling: first the center bay, next the south bay. Then it got dangerous. It had to come down.

How old was this sonabitch? Rick calls to my father, but Dad doesn't answer. His huge hands wave in the air, swatting the flies.

I didn't want it to be that alive, that full of family. I didn't want that excited grief rising at each pull. At last they tied a chain to the corner of the granary, where just that morning they had pried off the wall the entire collection of thirties, forties, fifties license plates—one for every car, tractor, and pickup they ever owned. They thrust the tines of the hi-

low right through the floor to lift out Grandpa's first winnowing machine, dead chaff still rolling out of its inner chamber.

The board they found had the old man's initials, and the date on it
told us it had been there a hundred years. I knew then how long people
had danced dot-to-dot among the pieces of light we are given in a place
this big with day in, day out seasons, hauling hay, feeding in winter, cats
born wild, ropes swinging, and then Patti explaining to her kids, *We
don't keep animals like this anymore, it's different now, and we need the
space—watch your step, there's nails popping everywhere.* Even the toddler stopped watching the birds dive and listened.

The corner of the granary must have been the piece in the puzzle
that made a house of cards out of a barn that had withstood a hundred
winters and two tornadoes. When the north end started leaning against
the silo, the men hitched both tractors to the inner post and snapped the
roof. Then it all came down, a great red hand slapping the ground, bil-
lowing the dust of old hay like ghosts of bleating cattle shuffling toward
us, and we cracked our knuckles while the barn swallows screamed and
dived for their broken nests.

About the Author

Anne-Marie Oomen grew up in Michigan's Oceana County (home of the National Asparagus Festival), east of the town of Hart and south of the village of Crystal Valley, on a small family farm in Elbridge Township, where she learned the dark and bright ways of her father's fields. She became a slightly better than average asparagus picker and a fair cherry picker, but she totally failed as a tractor driver. This led her to believe that perhaps she wasn't meant to spend her life on a farm. The realization did not change her love of the place, just her direction from it. After several false attempts to find her home in the world (a convent, several colleges, stints in Europe and Chicago), she decided teaching might be something that would allow her time to write and still be close to farms. Though the premise proved false, she discovered she liked teaching, particularly creative writing, and she has been doing so in high schools and colleges for the past twenty years. She is now chair of creative writing at Interlochen Arts Academy.

The farm where she grew up, now called "Oomen Farms," is a lively agribusiness that continues successfully under the management of her brothers, who grow a multitude of root and green crops, maintain orchards, and educate the next generation of farmers. One sister manages the Michigan Asparagus Research Farm in Oceana County, another is a lover and rider of fine horses. Her father, now in his eighties, still attends to work at the farm, and her mother continues to negotiate the family holidays, births, marriages, and all that matters.

Though Oomen has written extensively about rural life and the sense of place associated with that life, she has also written plays based on the history of Michigan and essays inspired by her experience building (with her husband, David Early) their own home. Her interest in farms is currently nurtured by Community Supported Agriculture, particularly "Sweeter Song Farm" in Leelanau County (of which she is a member) as well as her association with the Fresh Food Partnership, not to mention her return trips to the family farm, where twelve nieces and nephews keep her entertained and inspired. She and her husband live near an old orchard in Empire, Leelanau County, with two cats, Walt Whitman and Emily Dickinson.